TESTIMONIALS

As the field and all of the professionals of note would expect, Jeff Weld has provided us with more than a guide through American education as it rolls off the press in DC. Jeff's level of storytelling and discourse are always so magical, with this as no exception. The treat comes from being able to share Jeff's experiences through his own eyes. His mild manner, infectious smile, and brilliance make their way in exponentials throughout this work. A treat for us all and a piece for the generations following!

—Jan Morrison, Founder and CEO,
Teaching Institute for Excellence in STEM

Jeff Weld gives readers an unparalleled view of the Herculean effort to create the guiding document of the nation's STEM education movement in only 12 months. *Charting a Course for American Education... from out on a limb in the executive branch* masterfully demonstrates Weld's ability to build consensus among passionate factions while orchestrating an incomparably inclusive process in federal policymaking from which all can be inspired to answer the call of public service.

—Wes Hall, Executive Director, STEMx

A truly modern-day *Gulliver's Travels* in Bureaucracyland, Dr. Weld shares his larger-than-life experiences throughout this amazing book. You will find this to be a riveting firsthand account of the actual bureaucratic chaotic scenes documented by a true professional who feels passionately about STEM Education and gave his all to provide the leadership and expertise which he was appointed to accomplish, meeting and overcoming obstacles and roadblocks at every turn.

—Jo Anne Vasquez, PhD,
Arizona Transition Years' Teacher and Curriculum STEM Initiatives at the Helios Education Foundation, past president of the National Science Teachers Association and of the National Science Education Leadership Association

Charting a Course for American Education...from out on a limb at the executive branch is an inspiring and dizzying ride through the complex pathways of decision-making in Washington DC's corridors of power to create a groundbreaking framework for advancing STEM education. Jeff Weld's story is a triumphant mix of dedication, belief in an ideal, experience, superb negotiation and collaboration skills, and a healthy dose of "Iowa nice" to smooth policy bumps along the way. I highly recommend it.

—John Stiles, PhD, senior specialist, Southeast Asian Ministers of Education Organization (SEAMEO), and editor-in-chief, Southeast Asian Journal of STEM Education

Anyone who has seen the musical *Hamilton* will recall Aaron Burr's lament, "I wanna be in the room where it happens." Dr. Weld takes us on a journey into the rooms in which the "it" of federal science education policy work happens. Probably not all of the rooms, but enough to give readers casually familiar with the process of policy making sufficient insight to know whether or not they would really want to be in the rooms where it happens."

—Thomas Peters, Ed.D., Executive Director,
South Carolina Coalition for Mathematics & Science at Clemson University

Jeff Weld's spirited memoir tells the absorbing tale of his efforts to shepherd the nation's five-year plan for STEM education through Washington's labyrinthine bureaucracy--all at a time of rising political discord. Yet the real heroes of his story are the educators, researchers, community leaders and other state and local STEM champions whose wisdom, devotion, and hard-won expertise helped him shape the plan. Without them, he warns, any federal initiatives will wither on the vine.

—Claus von Zastrow,
Principal, Education Commission of the States

Weld takes readers through the dungeons-and-dragons game of policy-making in today's Washington, where the dungeons are the labyrinth of offices in and around the White House, and the dragons are the bureaucrats deeply dedicated to their agencies and causes. I recommend *Charting a Course for American Education...from out on a limb at the executive branch* to anyone interested in learning how policies and documents like America's Strategy for STEM Education go from idea to finished product.

—Alan Colburn, PhD, professor of science education at
California State University Long Beach

For all who aspire to change the world in authentic and heart-centered ways, this book is like having coffee with a mentor. Weld invites the reader to sit under a cherry blossom along the Potomac as he enthralls you with behind-the-scenes stories of how he navigated through a politically-charged climate to weave the disparate views of the nation's most prominent minds into trailblazing for America's STEM evolution. A must-read for passionate STEM educators and policymakers!

—Yen Verhoeven, PhD
CEO, Qi Learning Research Group

Jeff Weld's spirited memoir tells the absorbing tale of his efforts to shepherd the nation's five-year plan for STEM education through Washington's labyrinthine bureaucracy--all at a time of rising political discord. Yet the real heroes of his story are the educators, researchers, community leaders and other state and local STEM champions whose wisdom, devotion, and hard-won expertise helped him shape the plan. Without them, he warns, any federal initiatives will wither on the vine.

—Claus von Zastrow,
Principal, Education Commission of the States

Weld takes readers through the dungeons-and-dragons game of policy-making in today's Washington, where the dungeons are the labyrinth of offices in and around the White House, and the dragons are the bureaucrats deeply dedicated to their agencies and causes. I recommend *Charting a Course for American Education...from out on a limb at the executive branch* to anyone interested in learning how policies and documents like America's Strategy for STEM Education go from idea to finished product.

—Alan Colburn, PhD, professor of science education at
California State University Long Beach

For all who aspire to change the world in authentic and heart-centered ways, this book is like having coffee with a mentor. Weld invites the reader to sit under a cherry blossom along the Potomac as he enthralls you with behind-the-scenes stories of how he navigated through a politically-charged climate to weave the disparate views of the nation's most prominent minds into trailblazing for America's STEM evolution. A must-read for passionate STEM educators and policymakers!

—Yen Verhoeven, PhD
CEO, Qi Learning Research Group

CHARTING A COURSE FOR AMERICAN EDUCATION

from out on a limb
at the executive branch

CHARTING A COURSE FOR AMERICAN EDUCATION

from out on a limb
at the executive branch

Jeff Weld

Torchflame Books
Durham, NC

Copyright © 2021 Jeff Weld

Charting a Course for American Education: from out on a limb at the executive branch
Jeff Weld
www.WeldWrites.com
weldjeffrey@gmail.com

Published 2021, by Torchflame Books
an Imprint of Light Messages
www.lightmessages.com
Durham, NC 27713 USA
SAN: 920-9298

Paperback ISBN: 978-1-61153-416-0
E-book ISBN: 978-1-61153-417-7
Library of Congress Control Number: 2021901711

ALL RIGHTS RESERVED

No part of this publication may be reproduced, stored in a retrieval system, or transmitted in any form or by any means, electronic, mechanical, photocopying, recording, scanning, or otherwise, except as permitted under Section 107 or 108 of the 1976 International Copyright Act, without the prior written permission except in brief quotations embodied in critical articles and reviews.

This is a work of creative nonfiction. The events are portrayed to the best of the author's memory. While all the stories in this book are true, names and identifying details have been changed to protect the privacy of the people involved. Some of the characters are amalgams of actual people. Dates, dialogue, and settings are generalized re-creations. The conversations in the book all come from the author's recollections, though they are not meant to represent word-for-word transcripts. Rather, the author has retold them in a way that evokes the feeling and meaning of what was said, and in all instances, the essence of the dialogue is accurate.

To all the academic professionals
who risk reputations to answer the call
to serve our nation valiantly
in a political environment
sometimes averse to science and facts.

To all the academic professionals
who risk reputations to answer the call
to serve our nation valiantly
in a political environment
sometimes averse to science and facts.

CONTENTS

Who Is This book For? ii

Acknowledgments iii

1—Mission Accomplished 1

2—"Hello, This Is Bethany..." 13

3—A Day in the Life 30

4—Charting a Course 48

5—Of the People, by the People, and for the People of STEM ... 63

6—Cherry Blossoms and STEMs 81

7—Crossing the Rubicon 98

8—Other Duties as Assigned 121

9—Fourth-Quarter Crunch 137

10—Unplanned Encore 161

Epilogue 172

About the Author 175

WHO IS THIS BOOK FOR?

Charting a Course for American Education...from out on a limb at the executive branch is a modern-day Gulliver's Travels in Bureaucracyland. Readers get the guest chair in Office 442 on the fourth floor of the Eisenhower Executive Office Building on the White House grounds at 1650 Pennsylvania Avenue NW, through 2018 and most of 2019. An entertaining tale of trials and triumphs of a professor from a Midwest regional university, recruited to join a polarizing administration for a nonpartisan chore. It is part policy exposé, and part memoir.

For political science aficionados and wonks, it's a peek behind the curtains at the world of federal policymaking, albeit an atypically efficient instance. For fans of stories of conquest of the commoner against steep odds, there are nail-biting depths and dance-happy heights. For the memoir set, it's an autobiographical moment of a regular Joe from mid-America, dropped into the nation's political epicenter, knowing none of the rules, yet pulling off a nearly impossible task through perseverance more than brilliance.

For anyone involved in STEM education—school administrators, business leaders, policymakers, nonprofit directors, higher education officials—it's a rare glimpse into who set the course, and how. For educators, whether classroom, clubs, or community centers, it provides a baseline context for the direction these fields are taking.

Whichever your hook, welcome to the roller-coaster ride. This is an honest, open, entertaining, apolitical account of how an important education policy got done during a period of dysfunction.

ACKNOWLEDGMENTS

Many people went out on a limb for this story to happen. The whole remarkably unlikely and historic account is woven of, and by, individuals who took a chance, bore some burden, accepted the challenge, and sacrificed for the nation. It happened, and exists, because the leadership team at the Office of Science and Technology Policy (OSTP) took a big chance on an unknown prospect who might get them a product to fulfill a congressional mandate in an improbably narrow time window. I am eternally grateful to the people who brought me to the attention of the OSTP.

Another leader without whom this book would not exist is Iowa Governor Kim Reynolds, who saw the value in lending the governor's STEM director to a national project to share what we've learned, and to return smarter. And while I was away, my colleagues at the Council's operations center bore significant burden for this to happen. The governor's recruit from industry to take the helm in my absence performed magnificently, as did my teammates operating the STEM network across the state. Not only did they hold our ship of STEM steady in my absence, they navigated forward in a number of invigorating ways.

It was my new friends across federal agencies who climbed out on a limb, too, accepting the challenge to do something profound for America, undaunted by the unprecedented pace and the seismic shift from business as usual.

And finally, my family joined me out on the limb, sacrificing for the nation. Although what we did cannot hold a candle to the sacrifice of soldiers risking their lives in defense of the country, it would have been easy at our station in life—peak of career, comfort, friends, hobbies, routine, stability, and predictability—for those closest to me to advise that we decline this invitation to serve. But my sons, my siblings, my mother, and most importantly, my life partner, Mary, endorsed the gamble, despite some stark contrasts in political perspective with the occupants of the White House at the time. After thirty-plus years of marriage, one expects to know all there is to know about a spouse, but Mary surprised me yet again, revealing ever-deeper degrees of grit, adaptability, independence, and devotion—to me, to family, and to the nation. Thanks to her, and to all who took chances, bore burdens, accepted challenges, and made sacrifices, the STEM education community across the United States of America has a powerful North Star to chart a course forward.

Readers owe a debt of gratitude to the talented editor and wordsmither Julie Lipkin of Cape Cod, who transformed clunky prose into a lively jaunt. And English graduate student Zach Batt, at the University of Northern Iowa, sharpened his editing chops on it as well.

1

MISSION ACCOMPLISHED

An inquisition wasn't what I expected when venturing across the Potomac river to Alexandria one sunny spring morning in 2018. A conference room full of federal scientists, engineers, mathematicians, and computer scientists showed up for my visit to their agency. They were already assembled around the table as I was directed to the sole empty chair at the head. Chatter subsided, and several scooted forward to the edge of their chairs and leaned in, elbows on desktop, chins balanced on their folded hands.

Just who do we have here? was the question written on their faces.

Over the course of my first few months in the White House Office of Science and Technology Policy (OSTP), I was routinely invited to visit one federal agency or another, and jumped at each opportunity. Everyone was interested in how things were going on the development of a new federal STEM plan, eventually to be named *America's Strategy for STEM Education*, and I really needed their input.

In all, I answered the invitations of fourteen agencies—NASA, the National Oceanic and Atmospheric Administration, the Agriculture Department, the Departments of Energy and Education, the National Science Foundation, and eight others whose portfolios incorporated STEM education investments. This latest agency stop was deep into the process, though, with the bones of the new STEM strategy beginning to take on skeletal structure.

These feds had lots of questions, but little patience: Where did this draft plan come from? Who suggested such priorities? Who's conducting oversight and approvals? What guidelines are steering the project? Why deviate from the 2013 STEM plan?

I'd get as far as replying, "Well..." and "They..." and "If I could just..." before the next question arrived. The table was shrinking as my hosts got louder, closer.

Mercifully, after ninety minutes the interrogation ceased, and I promised to carefully consider all of their concerns. Everyone shuffled out, glancing back and murmuring. I lingered with the agency's division director, Pat, who'd invited me.

Welcome tweet from the White House OSTP in December 2017

"There's a lot of passion in that group," she said, once the room had cleared.

"Pat, it seems as though there might've been more than passion going on," I replied. "Do you think there's a political undercurrent to what went on here?"

Pat considered me for a bit, then whispered, "Well, to be honest, many in the room were likely not of your party."

I stepped back and extended my arms, palms up. "But I'm a registered Independent." As if they should've known.

Pat arched her brow in surprise. Squeezing my hand, she fixed her gaze upon mine.

"Then I don't know how on earth you got that job."

Fifteen months later, on the afternoon of Monday, September 23, 2019, at 4:30 p.m., I exited the wrought iron and heavily guarded west gate of the White House grounds, onto Pennsylvania Avenue for the 207th and final time. Dawdling tourists paused to look me up and down, while climate activists protesting that day's UN Climate Summit in New York City, crossed my path while trudging out of Lafayette Park across the street, in search of relief from the record-setting warmth—over ninety degrees on a day typically twenty degrees cooler. A stone's throw toward the southeast, the president of the United States was also feeling the heat while he sat in the Oval Office as the Ukraine arms-for-political-favor scandal broke that afternoon. By the next day, the US House of Representatives would launch his first impeachment inquiry. It was all a downer from the high I was on after bidding adieu to my teammates in the OSTP, up on the fourth floor of the Eisenhower Executive Office Building (EEOB).

Tourists to Washington, DC, cannot help but marvel at the massive and ostentatious EEOB, towering over the West Wing inside the perimeter fence at 1650 Pennsylvania Avenue. Its distinctive French Second Empire architecture is a curious departure from the Greek Revivalist style of the Treasury Building that mirrors its position at the White House's East Wing. Home to the pre-Pentagon War Department, its four floors now house an array of executive offices, including the Space Council, the vice president's office, the director of the Office of Management and Budget, the National Security Council, White House communications, and the OSTP. Much of the fourth floor is devoted to science and technology policy offices, including divisions on environment and energy, national security, science, and technology innovation—the division that included STEM education.

Over the course of my twenty-one months there, some serious business got done, including significant policy-guiding reports on artificial intelligence, space weather, ocean health, advanced manufacturing, quantum information science, medical imaging research, near-Earth object preparedness, cybersecurity, and of course, STEM education. Two layers below all of the drama constantly playing out in the Oval Office were sixty or so incredibly talented and driven people working well-past dusk, six or seven days a week, to provide Executive Office policy direction to agencies of the federal government. Sometimes that advice was taken, sometimes not. Yet people did their jobs.

I'd made my rounds and exchanged heartfelt farewells with the OSTP career staffers who worked there long enough to have seen innumerable short-timers like me come and go, as well as the political appointees in place just since the 2016 election (or more recently, in some cases—several of us were brought on board a year or two into the administration). They were an impressive lot—leading thinkers in their chosen fields—and I felt a twinge of guilt packing up for home. But my service to the nation was complete. In fact, my purpose for being in the building in the fall of 2019, after weeks back in Iowa, was to pass the baton to a successor at our monthly interagency STEM education coordination meeting. Two dozen agency professionals representing fifteen departments, among them Transportation and Labor, and such agencies as Environmental Protection and the National Institutes of Health, had been brought to Room 350 EEOB to discuss implementing the goals of the new federal STEM plan.

Many had contributed content to the plan over the course of a testy, vigorous, and intense 2018, so this was a comparatively gentle lift.

Anyone who's endured and persevered through a daunting challenge on a team given poor odds of success, only to prevail surprisingly and magnificently ahead of schedule, can appreciate my mixed feelings on closing that meeting. We'd crawled across the finish line and collapsed in an exhausted heap together. High-fives, hugs, and well-wishes all around. Someone had brought a bon voyage cake. It was a carnival ride that ended too early—exhilarating, with a touch of vertigo.

A warm send-off from the federal STEM committee at my last meeting as the full-time STEM advisor at the OSTP in late 2018.

A bit of congressional legislative context situates the policy miracle that took place in 2018. The 2010 reauthorization of the America COMPETES (Creating Opportunities to Meaningfully Promote Excellence in Technology, Education, and Science) Act, known as the ACA, had been signed by President Obama on January 4, 2011, and set my unlikely destiny in motion. The legislation directs the White House OSTP to establish an interagency committee from which a STEM education strategic plan would emerge and be updated every five years. The OSTP was to report to Congress annually on progress toward the plan's goals. In 2011, the OSTP's array of brilliant policy advisors on oceans, weather, medicine, weaponry, computation, ecology, space and other frontiers found themselves suddenly responsible for education policy as well.

More than two years after PL 111-358 was signed into law, May of 2013, the first federal STEM education five-year strategic plan was released by the OSTP as a product of the freshly established interagency Committee on STEM Education (CoSTEM). Details about that plan will be explored in subsequent chapters. For now, suffice to say that expert policy advisors on the frontiers of the sciences did a fairly good job of satisfying the COMPETES directive on STEM education, while leaving lots of opportunity for improvement. An update of that plan would become due in 2018, under a new administration. That would be my baby.

On the heels of the election of November 2016, the OSTP leaders appointed by President Obama were swept into the streets of D.C. I knew many of them by legend, and a couple by casual association, and have enormous respect for their work in science and technology. Such turnover, whoever the presidents are exchanging the baton, is enormously disruptive for science and technology policy in the USA. The 2021 presidential transition set a new bar in that regard. The career staffers who smooth over election transitions are national treasures.

As of noon, on January 20, 2017, a real-estate tycoon turned reality TV star somehow elected president took office, and the repopulating of the OSTP was probably not a priority, judging by the time frame for rebuilding. The delay in standing up the office was exacerbated by a blindsiding of the career staffers by such an unlikely election outcome. Career staff told me they'd already begun to work with Hillary's transition team in mapping out office spaces and planning appointments. Most overwhelmed may have been the members of the new president's transition team. They probed their tentacles into the federal science and technology universe, pulling loaner experts from other agencies into the OSTP. Likely, they also tapped channels of the party machine to identify leading thinkers who were available and politically aligned.

I met some from both pools. Having arrived too late for the start-up phase, I'd heard about the whirlwind period of rebuilding dozens of offices with thousands of appointees. I'd venture to guess that the Council of Economic Advisors, the Office of the United States Trade Representative, the National Security Council, the Domestic Policy Council, and others more directly supporting the policies of the newly elected administration, got stood up first. My installation would be almost a year later, the culmination and personification of an unorthodox protocol of an unusual administration.

With verve and earnestness did colleagues from many federal agencies remind me early upon my arrival in 2018, of the COMPETES Act language requiring an "update" as opposed to an overhaul of the 2013 STEM plan. The goals and strategies were so familiar to those who had crafted the original that they had little appetite for a complete rewrite. The 2013 plan validated and reinforced the existing activities and emphases of each federal agency, especially the major players—the National Science Foundation, the Department of Education, the National Institutes of Health, and the Department of Defense. The 2013 plan supported a standard fare of undergraduate and graduate STEM education research and programming, and did not rock their boats. But it did precipitate a well-intentioned, though radioactive, realignment of funds and functions at the cost of minor agencies, including the US Geological Survey, the Oceanic and Atmospheric Administration, Environmental Protection, and the Departments of Agriculture and Energy.

The wariness with which I was initially regarded by some at the minor agencies didn't make sense. Until a pattern emerged. The same question kept coming up—something along the lines of, *Are you going to cut our funding again?* That led me to hold conversations with Management and Budget officials and former OSTP leaders that eventually revealed an autopsy of sorts for what I began to call The Massacre of 2014.

It turned out that to comply with COMPETES, the OSTP had worked with the budget office to orchestrate a federal-wide inventory of STEM education activities and spending across thirteen agencies. It revealed that 226 programs collectively spent about $3 billion a year. Authors of the 2013 plan wrote on page 6 that uncoordinated federal spending had spawned a proliferation of STEM programs. True enough—similar and redundant programs for teachers, students, postdocs, undergraduates, and others had popped up in various agencies, with little cross talk or collaboration. The answer was to introduce into the 2013 STEM plan, a coordination goal for greater effectiveness and efficiency. To do so, the OSTP and the inter-agency committee on STEM designated some agencies as "lead," and others as "collaborating," with the objective of "consolidating" programs and "aligning investments with roles and missions."

In reality, all that good intention manifested as funds diverted from one agency to another, programs consolidated, and in a few instances, simply cut. Big winners, as dictated by the 2013 plan, were the Department of Education (designated lead on all things related to STEM instruction), the National Science Foundation (lead on all undergraduate STEM programs), and the Smithsonian Institution (lead on public engagement programs). Some of those who lost funding and programs were NASA, the Oceanic and Atmospheric Administration, the Agriculture Department, the Geological Survey, and Environmental Protection.

The idea of coordination made lots of sense. But in practice, it pitted agency against agency. The number of STEM programs was shaved by about fifty. Interestingly though, spending did not decrease. It just shifted. Coordination and collaboration diminished in a toxic environment of distrust. Agencies creatively shielded their programs from the ax by renaming them to keep them off the inventory.

Thus, I had two strikes already upon stepping up to the plate in 2018, to lead development of a new federal STEM education plan: winners from the 2013 plan were uninterested in changing it, while losers from the 2014 Massacre were still hair-trigger mad and suspicious of anybody dropping in from Pennsylvania Avenue to snoop into their business.

Aside from the land mines lying in wait, STEM policy leadership at the OSTP would be a tough act to follow in the wake of Obama appointees and activities. STEM education had been a very active division under the watch of then director John Holdren. Staffing had been two or three times what it was upon my arrival. A few months into the job, an Obama-era staffer came up to visit me in the Eisenhower Building.

"When I was in here," he swept his arm across the sparsely populated office suite, "this whole wing was packed. You could hardly walk down the hall for all the desks lining both sides."

That must've been nice, I said.

"Eh, in one way you have it lots better. There were so many people with so many agendas, and so many layers of clearances that it was hard to get things done. You, on the other hand, have direct access to the director."

Those words turned out to be prescient.

Still, Holdren's team had produced celebrated White House science fairs every year. It had started the STEM Master Teacher Corps; launched the Change the Equation and Educate to Innovate campaigns; injected tons of momentum into the maker movement, which focuses on promoting invention and creativity; embedded a STEM priority into the Department of Education's Race to the Top competition; and proposed significant STEM education investments in annual budgets. And it was President Obama, who signed the COMPETES Act into law, created the interagency Committee on STEM and all that came of it, including a five-year strategic plan.

To top it all off, one of the last bills he had signed as president, on January 6, 2017, was the American Innovation and Competitiveness Act, creating a new STEM Education Advisory Panel of interested Americans to oversee and advise federal agencies on STEM programming, policies, and outcomes. I was a big fan.

For all their science fairs, presidential proclamations, new commissions, and legislation, and for so many distinguished pedigrees the likes of Yale, MIT, Princeton, Stanford, Duke, Brown, and Harvard populating the OSTP, they missed their biggest STEM opportunity. While the STEM strategy was unfolding from 2011 to 2013, on Pennsylvania Avenue, STEM networks of schools, businesses, higher education institutions, nonprofits, zoos, museums, scout troops, and all sorts of STEM stakeholders were bubbling up across the USA at levels ranging from local communities to statewide networks to national consortia. These nascent STEM ecosystems throughout the country were reinventing the same wheels due to the lack of a leading entity. No leadership on STEM education was coming from DC. To have seized the opportunity to inform and inspire an organic grassroots movement by engaging STEM trailblazers from Tulsa to Tampa to Terre Haute, and all points in between, would have saved countless hours and dollars spent on trial-and-error discovery. Their voices were not heard while the 2013 federal STEM plan was being produced. The product, as a result, had little, if any, relevance or impact beyond the I-495 beltway.

Just before I arrived to the OSTP in late 2017, the Department of Education's new administration committed $200 million to STEM education, with a focus on computer science. The impetus had been a White House gathering of Silicon Valley executives who, together, committed to match the investment.

Some of my associates perceived the assignment of the dollars to that agency as illogical (they being of other agencies). Their criticism was that STEM education was not native to the US Department of Education, and that a disciplinary niche grant program would've been more appropriately assigned to an agency that owns STEM education, such as NASA or the National Science Foundation. But the new administration had nowhere to go for advice, given that the interagency Committee on STEM Education had disbanded after the 2016 election, and had not yet been rechartered. Nor was there STEM expertise at the OSTP. Finally, in 2017, the Education Department came out with new strategic priorities, one of which was STEM. By 2018, a grant competition was put together to get the $200 million spent. In 2019, the awards were announced, though the promised corporate match was no where to be seen.

My first conversations with the OSTP team in the fall of 2017, revealed an abundance of STEM-focused thinking, if not activity. Lots of talk, no action. Education reform and worker training were on their minds, but how STEM might fit had yet to be determined. Earlier that year, in April of 2017, the president had signed an executive order that prohibits federal interference with State and local control over education. Another executive order came down two months later to expand apprenticeships. The next year, halfway through my tenure, the administration established the President's National Council for the American Worker. And a few weeks later, in July 2018, it ushered through Congress a tweaked law, the Career and Technical Education for the 21st Century Act, otherwise known as the Perkins Reauthorization.

It was in this environment that a new STEM strategic plan would incubate. Observers would witness a marked shift in emphasis toward workforce preparation, from the traditional academic thrust under President Obama. Aside from that stratospheric level of guidance, I had a blank slate and a frequent, if not too helpful, "You're the expert" deference to keep the administration compliant with the COMPETES Act, and to produce a STEM plan. In one year.

Charting a Course for Success: America's Strategy for STEM Education debuted 358 days after my arrival at the OSTP. All that remains is to peel back the screen and go behind the scenes for the who, what, when, where, a bit more why, and how.

Last day at the OSTP, gutter-balled in presidential bowling alley

2

"HELLO, THIS IS BETHANY..."

I was pulling into a Quik Stop on the way to Cherokee, Iowa, for a STEM event one blustery September afternoon in 2017, when area code 202 buzzed my Motorola.

"Hello, this is Bethany Lee at the White House, calling for Jeff Weld, please."

Something one is not prepared to hear. I struggled to focus on steering the car away from the gas pumps, pulling up to the storefront a little uncontrolled, tires rebounding off the curb.

"Hi, this is Jeff. What can I do for you?" I shifted into park, muted NPR, and killed the motor.

"It's great to catch you, Jeff. We've heard a lot about your work in Iowa, and would like to ask you about STEM."

It was not unprecedented—since 2011, my state's STEM project had garnered attention from numerous other states, and even a couple nations. We'd built a strong array of programs, and a transparent evaluation system that won admiration externally, and legislative support internally, year after year. Just a month earlier, I'd published a book about it—*Creating a STEM Culture*. Maybe they'd seen it.

"Of course, Bethany. But out of the gates, I have to ask how it is that the White House is curious about STEM in Iowa. I need some context."

"Well, to be more specific, I'm with the Office of Science and Technology Policy—the OSTP. We're part of the executive branch. Heard of us?"

Most definitely I had. Epic reports and policy directives come out of the OSTP, penned by a who's who of the S&T world. It's home to the President's Council of Advisors on Science and Technology—PCAST—whose work I'd studied religiously. In 2014, the council had issued a landmark analysis on educational technology. In 2011, it had produced a report titled *Engage to Excel,* which challenged higher education systems to produce more STEM graduates. In 2010, it had issued a seminal K–12 science and math reform treatise called *Prepare and Inspire,* focused on making and keeping excellent teachers. In between, it cranked out trendsetting guidebooks on nanotechnology, vaccines, renewable energy, cybersecurity, bioweaponry, and just about every other hot topic that is brain candy for geeks and nerds. Oh, yes, the OSTP is the big leagues to everyone in my business.

"Yes, of course. I'm a fan of the office." I struggled to portray chill, despite churning adrenaline. "And I'm so glad you're interested in STEM. Where should we start?"

Where Bethany wanted to begin was with my experience in workforce development. Over the course of ninety minutes (blowing right through the Cherokee rendezvous I'd set out for that morning), she quizzed me on how to solve the technical workforce skills gap, how to meet demand for more teachers in S&T, how to drive change in higher education to respond to shifts in workforce demand, and other challenges we STEM-ers take on daily. It was an intellectual batting cage with speedballs aimed at my head.

By evidence of two more phone calls, each more specific and pointed toward federal policy ideas, I guessed that I'd apparently not whiffed or fouled off her pitches.

Phone call number 3, a couple weeks later, ended with Bethany asking, "Do you know anyone who could come advise the White House on STEM education policy?"

I should have seen this coming, but did not, figuring that, like others who had called to discuss STEM education, they simply sought policy brainstorming. And even had I the foresight, I would've still answered the same way. My current post directing Iowa's STEM program was a perfect fit, and DC was a polarized circus I wanted no part in.

"Oh, what a great opportunity, Bethany. Yes I do." I reached across my desk for a copy of my 2017 book on STEM, and thumbed to Chapter 9—an array of closing briefs submitted by seventeen leading STEM friends. "Right here and now I could give you more than a dozen names of people who'd be excellent."

"Yes, well, thanks, Jeff. But we're hoping you might consider joining us."

What would prepared even look like for such an invitation?

"Wow, that is an incredible prospect to consider, but I'll need to think about it." I asked her to give me a few days to ponder.

―᠊᠊᠊᠊ᴡᴡ᠊᠊᠊᠊―

What had gone on inside the OSTP leading up to this offer, I've pieced together based on what my then-future colleagues would tell me, along with observations of other new hires.

Stating the obvious, this was an unusual administration. Unlike more typical new presidents who come out of Congress or governorship, these folks were not well-connected in DC. No deep ties, legacy networks, or party connections to access pools of talent. And carryover from the previous administration would be minimal. This was a clean sweep (with the exception an undersecretary of state, an assistant secretary of the Treasury, an acting director of DEA—the Drug Enforcement Administration—plus a few others who'd made the transition, only to get axed early on by Number 45).

Thus, many leadership positions across the executive offices were interim appointments drawn from the president's own business connections (the acting director of the OSTP, for example), and from campaign staff, as well as the poaching of talent from friendly governors. Lots of bright, young ambitious appointees found themselves in potently influential positions.

Fortunately for the OSTP, its young and ambitious political science major (now acting director) was acutely aware of the mammoth responsibility he'd been handed. Rapidly peopling the office with experts to inform White House policy on the significant S&T issues of our times, he leaned heavily on the federal agencies, borrowing their scientists, engineers, and technologists with policy expertise on temporary assignments called *detail*. Some of the smartest, most dedicated and nonpolitical public servants I have ever had the honor of meeting came to the OSTP on detail from Defense, the NSF, the National Institute of Standards and Technology, OMB, and elsewhere. Some stayed just long enough to bridge an issue until the administration was able to go out and recruit someone of its own brand. Others have stayed on for the long haul. When it came to STEM education, the administration clearly wanted to go off campus, despite the presence of numerous feds of deep and wide expertise in the area. While likely unsure just what they wanted, the political leaders knew change was going to be needed.

By the accounts of insiders who answered my "Why me?" the administration took a businesslike approach, just getting on the phone and asking around. Obviously, those tasked with filling the spot did not prioritize Ivy League pedigree or membership in the National Academy. Nor does their choice lead one to believe that prior national policy experience was a must-have. And surprisingly, membership in the Grand Old Party wasn't a prerequisite.

What I was told by friends in the STEM sphere who'd been contacted was that Bethany and leaders at the OSTP asked two simple questions of people: "Who's doing great work in STEM education right now?" and "Who wrote the book on STEM?"

That's a fresh and unorthodox approach for DC. Had those two questions been asked back in 2010, during round one of federal STEM strategic planning, the complexion of the report, and the people working on it, might've been different. With enormous respect due scientists and policy professionals in charge at that time, they had not walked in the shoes of STEM educators. A state STEM leader out of a regional university from the heart of America, whose frontline scars and triumphs built authentic expertise, was a brilliant choice in its practicality. To this day, I can name a dozen people who would've fit the bill. So I strove to channel the wisdom of each of them.

An offer of the highest job in my field was on the table, a pinnacle post that caps the most distinguished of careers—to advise the office of the president of the United States on one's niche specialty. An offer, sight unseen. The haste was unsettling. The unknowns about these people, what chores they had in mind, and by what terms we might engage made the offer prematurely, preposterously undercooked. I called Bethany to suggest we arrange a visit.

"We don't really have the budget to bring you out for an interview, Jeff."

That was hard to believe.

"Nor do we have the time for a drawn-out decision."

That was more convincing.

"But if you wish to come out, like, next week, we'd be happy to sit down and fully discuss the appointment."

As chance would have it (a phrase that could pepper this whole saga), I was scheduled in Baltimore for a conference the next week. So we set up a date, and I hopped a train from the Inner Harbor to DC, on October 6, 2017. I arrived an hour early and skated through prearranged security. Each floor of the Eisenhower Executive Office Building is a big square of immaculately polished black and white checkered marble and limestone tiles that covers a half-mile. I logged over two miles wandering all four floors, plus stairways, and still had time for a cocoa in the basement cafeteria before our 10:00 a.m. fourth-floor meetup.

Circling the table in the OSTP director's office were the president's interim director; his communications lead and congressional liaison; another appointee from the Domestic Policy Council downstairs, who'd recently worked on the $200 million STEM investment to the Department of Education; and several career staffers, including the OSTP's chief of staff and legal counsel, who'd been there through several presidents. I was bummed that Bethany was not present, but came to learn that her status, administrative assistant, was a notch below the pecking order of people in the room.

It was more of a grilling than I'd expected, given that I'd already had the offer over the phone. This meeting was my idea, after all, so I figured on doing most of the quizzing. But they were locked and loaded from the moment we sat down, with asks born of genuine curiosity ("How did STEM rise so fast to be such a big deal across states?"), and questions more typical of an interview ("What do you think the federal government ought to do to support STEM education?").

My STEM book was just a few weeks old by then, so I merely parroted it. Chapter 2 covered the rise of STEM. Chapter 3 explored the feds' role: "How could we hasten school-business partnerships?" Chapter 4: "What do the nation's colleges need to do?" Chapter 7—the last question, from the chief of staff, had no anchor in the book: "What do you know about crafting federal policy?"

If that's a deal breaker, so be it. "I know STEM, and you know policy. Isn't that how this place works?"

By the time I caught a plane for home that night, an offer was on the table: senior policy advisor and assistant director, STEM education, Office of Science and Technology Policy, Executive Office of the President. The unimaginably far-fetched had become a tangible possibility. Excitement, intrigue, honor, and duty were counterbalanced by loyalty to my STEM team back in Iowa, instability and discord at the White House, fear of how friends and family (most of whom aligned with the ousted party) would react, concern for my academic reputation, and most of all, family upheaval.

The next morning, I took a chance to discreetly field test the concept on a friend—a retired teacher and former state legislator of the Democratic stripe. We connected for a tailgate party preceding the University of Iowa versus Illinois football game on the morning of October 7th.

"Jerry, can I ask you something that would need to stay between us?"

He perked up. "Sure, of course."

"This'll be hard to believe, but I got a job offer from the White House."

Saying it out loud on a driveway in Iowa City sounded ridiculous. Jerry's jaw dropped, and his eyes popped.

Then he frowned. "To do what, for God's sake?"

I dove into the details of the post as best as I knew them to be. He wondered about the terms—duration, pay, living arrangements, and so on—all of which I said was unknown. What I mainly wanted was his opinion about accepting such a role at this time in history, considering his disdain for the current president.

"Look,"—he took hardly any time to think about this—"you'd have to be comatose to pass on this. I don't care who the president is. It's a chance to shape STEM for the country, for Pete's sake."

We headed toward the stadium, Jerry scratching his head, repeating, "Jeesh."

Our Hawkeyes won the game handily, and I went home to poll my family—sons and daughter-in-law, siblings, and mother, most of whom ardently play for the blue team. Like Jerry, they were unequivocally supportive, despite personal misgivings over the administration. My colleagues on the state STEM team were initially less enthusiastic when asked opinions, not necessarily on political grounds, but based on disruption of operations.

Ultimately, their sentiments, expressed mostly through silence and sighs, were captured by one teammate's begrudging summation: "You'd be crazy not to take it."

There are more people in Greater Cleveland than in all of Iowa. Yet this breadbasket bullseye was amply represented in the 2018 White House. Our former governor, who launched Iowa's STEM program in 2011, was plucked to serve as ambassador to China. Iowa's secretary of agriculture became an undersecretary at the USDA. The lieutenant governor's press secretary went to the Department of Energy as director of public affairs. Several former staffers at the governor's office went to work in media and state relations offices of the executive branch. And of course, many Americans may recall the former acting Attorney General Matt Whitaker, an Iowan who succeeded Jeff Sessions for a few contentious winter months in 2018–2019. Apparently, we were trusted stock.

The 1939 movie *Mr. Smith Goes to Washington,* wove a storyline that was remarkably prescient of modern politics. A Midwestern governor who must pick a successor for a deceased senator, opts for a corruptible bumpkin, Jeff Smith, who defies assumptions to endure political countercurrent on the way to upending the status quo. Aside from our first names, our geographic origins, and our endurance to prevail despite interparty rancor, the parallels break down. Mr. Smith took a train to DC. I was chauffeured through a thousand-mile snowstorm by my brave spouse, Mary, while onboarding the new job from the passenger seat. Jeff Smith found love in the capital city, while my love—who never batted an eye about sending me east for this gig, nor about navigating slippery Interstate 76 through the Allegheny Mountains—dropped me off and went back to our dog, our house, our friends, and our family. Mr. Smith found housing right away—a hotel near the Capitol. I, too, found a hotel, on L Street NW, just four blocks from the White House. But unlike the senator, I'd eventually receive an expense allowance to offset housing and other expenses. (Much to my surprise, members of Congress don't get housing allowance, though they can live on campaign funds.) Washington, DC, is one of the most costly places to live, especially to be within a mile or two of the White House.

As it was by then mid-December, my timing was off for finding a vacant rental while the hotel tab piled up—until one day, an ideal apartment showed up on Craigslist. Too good to be true, it was a beautifully furnished one-bedroom, with a balcony, laundry, fitness center and pool, in a modern condominium on New Hampshire Avenue NW, just a half-mile from 1650 Pennsylvania Avenue. The typical price tag on units of this caliber started around $3,000 a month. But this guy—using the name Barack, wouldn't you know—asked just $1,650. For such a low price, he texted from area code 202, that a deposit of two months' rent into his bank was needed right away, because naturally, several others were interested, too. Desperate to settle, intensely busy by day, and proud to unearth an incredible bargain, I transferred a deposit to the account provided by Barack. And then the text messages stopped. The ad disappeared from Craigslist. *Poof.* Days later, a Capitol police detective told me this is all too common in DC, and they cannot catch these people, who are likely overseas somewhere.

One more commonality with Mr. Smith—we're both bumpkins.

After a visit home for the holidays, we optimistically loaded lamps, utensils, and a few furnishings and essentials into Mary's SUV to once again brave winter weather through the interstates of the eastern USA. Backs against the wall, paying seasonal premium hotel rates, we had to find me a place.

On the evening of January 2, 2018, after trudging through slush all day, visiting units culled from Apartments.com (Craigslist was now dead to me), we'd begun to lose hope in finding anything affordable. Where we're from, a four-thousand-square-foot mansion on an acre could be had for what these Capitol-ites were paying for seven hundred square feet within walking distance of the Metro.

We rounded the corner to our Courtyard Marriott, and as chance would have it...*ahem*... a high-rise on the periphery of George Washington University, just three blocks from the Eisenhower Building, proclaimed, *Now Renting. Affordable!,* on a banner over the portico.

While I was in the OSTP on the 3rd, my gal went and sealed the deal on a no-frills, fifth-floor efficiency cost-modulated by city rent-control rules. That night, we raided a Goodwill store and Target to make it livable. Mary departed the next day, and I dove deep into the work at hand now that my refuge had been established.

The year 2018 had eight government shutdowns and near-shutdowns saved by continuing resolutions. Shutdowns are colossally disruptive and disheartening. And they're rare when both the White House and Congress are controlled by the same party. Yet my first shutdown came just a few weeks in at the OSTP, on January 20, 2018.

The dispute was over immigration policy and funding for a wall along the border with Mexico. We all received strict orders from the White House personnel office on Friday afternoon, the 19th, that we could come into the office the next morning to secure our workspaces, but must be out within four hours—and don't come back until government reopens. It's a $5,000 fine, and possibly grounds for dismissal, to work during a shutdown. My colleagues and I joined 692,900 federal workers furloughed through that brief period. We all got paid when business resumed.

The difficult thing about a shutdown is you don't know how long it'll last. There'd been a sixteen-day shutdown in 2013, under President Obama, that the careerists remembered well. A twenty-one-day shutdown during the Clinton administration was recollected by only a few federal servants. I was on a clock to complete my mission within 365 days, so it was infuriating to sit around apartment 505 for three of them, unable to progress, and unable to jump on a plane for home, given that government could open at any time.

I'd entered the OSTP in December of 2017, under a continuing resolution—commonly referred to as a CR—to keep government operating. That one expired on December 22, but a shutdown was averted by a continuing resolution on *that* resolution that would keep government operating until January 19, 2018. That shutdown lasted from Saturday to Monday, so not much harm done. Again, on February 9th, the government shut down over disagreements on raising the debt ceiling. But differences were resolved by the next morning. Another CR was passed in March. A total of five CRs were passed that fiscal year. Strange way to operate a country.

The granddaddy shutdown of them all happened at the end of my appointment, on December 22, 2018. Another impasse over funding for a wall between Mexico and the USA. By then, I'd already escaped for Iowa, having transitioned to a part-time consulting role with the OSTP. The respite was most welcome, but I felt deep empathy for my federal friends and colleagues who were furloughed, or for those deemed "essential personnel" compelled to work, with only hope for pay through the thirty-five-day shutdown that finally ended on January 25, 2019. I was back out to DC shortly thereafter, beginning a monthly consultancy stint through most of 2019.

I was disabused of any fanciful notions regarding lottery-level payday back in the negotiation phase in fall 2017. We all know that no one gets rich by taking a public service job in Washington. At least, no one who's honest.

The pay cap in the OSTP in 2018 was $187,000. My income out east would be bound by the fact that we were agreeing to a one-year loan from my position directing the Iowa governor's STEM program. A deal was struck by which my salary and benefits would be maintained at the Iowa level, supplanted by an annual grant coming from the National Science Foundation (NSF) on behalf of the White House. A common practice at NSF, this agreement under the Intergovernmental Personnel Act made the hire much swifter for the administration—and safer for me. Basically, it constituted a leave of absence, rather than a resignation from my tenured university professorship and governor's post.

That is how the NSF became my employer of record, providing an office and a supervisor, who assigned me over to the White House OSTP full-time, on detail. The downside to being detailed is the redundancy in reporting, security clearances and background checks, double the passwords to retain for online systems, and door keypad accesses, staff meetings, cybersafety and ethics briefings, etc. I had two bosses spanning the Potomac River—one who called the shots (OSTP), and the other who dutifully carried out administrative functions (NSF).

The first sign of confusion springing from redundancy arose with my background check. Both the NSF and the Executive Office of the President dispatched FBI agents to conduct security clearances. Two separate agents came to my OSTP office for interviews, each ignorant of the other's inquiry. Neither cared. They asked the same things: Ever had run-ins with the law? Any overseas investments? Any family or friends involved in nefarious acts? Ever defaulted on a loan? Ever displayed any anti-American behaviors? Any other children besides the two I'd reported on the e-QIP form? (the Electronic Questionnaire for Investigations Processing is an extensive questionnaire all federal employees in sensitive positions must complete ahead of coming onboard. Quoting from the e-QIP, "Because the position for which you are being considered is one of public trust or is sensitive, your trustworthiness is a very important consideration in deciding your suitability for placement or retention in the position.") I wondered if the president and his family had each completed the e-QIP.

Based on the reports of my friends back home, only one FBI agent was sent to Iowa. Interviewed were the president of my university, my next-door neighbor, a close friend, and—oh, yes—the manager of my apartment building back in DC. My neighbor said she was asked if we appear to live beyond our means. Do we travel overseas much? Do we go through lots of cars or boats? My buddy was asked about my moral character—would I cheat or accept a bribe? The landlord assured him I was a squeaky clean tenant who paid rent on time and hosted no parties.

I must have passed their test of my "adherence to security requirements, honesty and integrity, vulnerability to exploitation or coercion, falsification, misrepresentation, and any other behavior, activities, or associations that tend to show the person is not reliable, trustworthy, or loyal" (quoting from the e-QIP). I've never been sure that I needed Top Secret security clearance, having never attended a secret meeting. Nor am I sure I was granted the status—no certificate or badge arrived in the mail. A secretary at the OSTP once hollered down the hall that, by the way, she thought I'd been granted Top Secret security clearance.

Nearly every week featured a required briefing at one or both offices. I came to know well the Blue Route of the Washington, DC, regional Metro rail system, jumping on at McPherson Square north of the White House, tunneling under the Potomac to the King Street station in Alexandria, for a short walk to NSF. Cybersafety updates constituted the briefing du jour there. Back at the OSTP, weekly briefings were much more intense, on topics including conflicts of interest, perils of personal email (if tapped for a Freedom of Information request, the office can search personal email if I'd used it even once for work), emergency protocols, chain of command, name tags, and travel advisories.

At one security briefing at the Eisenhower Building, an officer of the US Secret Service cautioned us on the vulnerabilities of our cell phones to be hijacked as listening devices. He demonstrated how downloading a simple app such as Super-Bright Flashlight reveals to unidentifiable third parties our location, network details, IP address, search history, camera-phone, and other applications access, all to which we mindlessly grant permission by accepting the terms upon download without reading those terms. *Gulp.* I used that app all the time.

Another briefing covered communicating information. They hammered into our heads the perils of conducting White House business on our personal email accounts—a legacy of the incendiary 2016 election battle, I reckoned. The same briefing also trained us to remove our identification badges immediately upon exiting the White House gates. The incidents they used to burn that into our brains had to do with front-page news stories, by enterprising reporters who'd tail the unmistakably name-badged Executive Office employees to coffee shops to eavesdrop on sensitive conversations.

The most sobering of briefings had to do with emergency protocols. They were stark reminders of the epicenter we inhabited—the risks of being in the crosshairs of bad actors, which we accepted alongside the thrill of charting a course for America. Shelter in place. Evacuate. Fire, chemical, bomb, active shooter defenses. Secret Service conducted periodic drills. A couple times, it was no drill. A fellow once set himself afire out front on Pennsylvania Avenue. Another time, a woman rammed the east gates outside the Eisenhower Building, with her minivan. Both resulted in lengthy lockdowns. There have been more than twenty security breaches since 2015, often by people suffering mental illness. I happened to be off the grounds for every breach and drill, but kept a full snack drawer in case.

The deck was stacked against this appointment early on: bilked for thousands on Craigslist; a spinning compass at the OSTP under a drama-driven White House; resistant feds clinging to STEM strategies of the previous administration, their guards up against snooping newcomers wielding a budget ax; and government-wide dysfunction ever-teetering toward shutdown. For all of this, I'd traded in a post atop the food chain back home: a rich network of peers changing the state; a dedicated team; unwavering support of my institution and governor; happy family, predictable calendar. More stark a contrast it could not have been. Weeks in, I'd grapple with hesitancy, solitude, second-guessing and self-doubt, guilt and regret for taking this on, and loneliness.

Two things kept the wind in my sails. First, were the random and unforeseen nods of appreciation. Etched indelibly into my dendrites are the faces and names of visitors to 442 Eisenhower Executive Office Building, who'd come up to share their STEM education perspectives, and in so doing, would offer encouragement that I lapped up like a parched desert wanderer, hopeful it didn't show.

"Thanks for doing this. For being here," said an administrator from the University of California system.

"We appreciate your service," said an officer from the National Guard—a particularly touching and humbling gesture.

"I'm so grateful, and so are my members, that you were appointed," said the director of a national education organization to which I belong. He'd confessed to worrying what this administration might do, and told me how surprised he was that they "got this one right."

Such comments, though not frequent, were periodic enough to sustain me. Outwardly, I'd deflect it. But the inward glow would endure through days of rough seas.

Second, were trips home—though they occurred months before the existence of a fund to help with the expenses of the trips. After that first Christmas back home, in 2017, Mary and I would rendezvous at STEM conferences and events in such places as Atlanta, Austin, and DC, until a quarter of the way through 2018, by which point we were running up quite a travel tab. I lamented to my NSF handler,

Pat, how imperfect a deal we'd struck for failing to get me home now and then.

"If your trips home were somehow essential to continuing your academic work," she said, "then we could help you."

"Ah, well, yes. Whatever it takes!" I replied.

Certainly, that'd be part of my mission home—to perpetuate the STEM work that continued to churn in my absence.

"In that case, just submit an independent research-development plan,"—known as an IR/D—"and get up to twelve trips home each year."

Bingo. I charted out three-week intervals to the remaining twenty-seven or so weeks remaining in the appointment, and carved them into the calendar. The IR/D became a sanity saver. Yet at the end of each of those long weekends back in Iowa, upon exiting the car at the airport for three more weeks in DC, I'd ask, "Do I really have to go back?"

"Yes. Get out!" Mary would say, through tears.

By September, this routine became a running gag, the tears subsiding. But earlier in 2018, I wasn't kidding, and she wasn't as resolute. The STEM education universe owes her for pushing me out of the car.

Every minute on the job at the OSTP tick-tocked through my brain, marking progress on the mission. Every night, by letter, email, or phone, I'd rate the day for family or a friend, as a big step forward or a baby step. Or once in an infuriating while, a wasted day, by that metric. No one in DC, except me, believed a new federal STEM strategy could be done inside of a year—and really, what did I know? *Give me two weeks in a quiet room, and out will pop a new strategic plan.*

It turns out that was naïve hubris. Jobs piled on. My scope of work expanded daily. The main task itself grew exponentially more complex. On top of that, anytime Congress produced draft STEM legislation, which happened surprisingly frequently, I was the administration's expert consultant. When G-7 and G-20 summits came around, my advice was sought on international education and workforce items. There were talking points to write for the OSTP leaders headlining conferences. There were incessant policy meetings on quantum, nanotech, cyber, medical, advanced manufacturing, oceans, and every other imaginable frontier in science and technology, each inviting the STEM guy's input on its talent pipelines. I felt like a pack mule getting loaded for expedition—everyone on the journey throwing gear on my back. They'll know capacity when the mule falls over.

Back in November of 2017, paperwork had included a short list of duties—a "major charge," and "minor charges."

Major charge:

- Lead a large, ambitious full-time dynamic interagency five-year strategic plan development for STEM, working closely with NSF, NASA, NOAA, NIH, the Departments of Education, Energy, Commerce, and Defense, the Patent and Trademark Office, Standards and Technology, the National Science and Technology Council, and others.

Minor charges:

- Coordinate and lead the STEM aspects of the NSTC through an interagency Committee on STEM Education, supported by working groups, on topics like computer science, diversity, K-12, postsecondary, etc. Evaluate the need for, and expansion or sunset, of working groups.

- Help with public events of the OSTP, such as the White House Science Fair, Astronomy Night, etc.

- Produce an annual report on accomplishments and progress.

Most of that, and then some, ended up coming true. But it was almost halfway through the appointment, in May of 2018, before an official duty roster came down, consisting of four expectations:

I. Summative report on 2013 STEM Strategic Plan, to Congress by summer.

II. Lead the production of 2019 STEM Strategic Plan, by fall.

III. Lead White House STEM events.

IV. Provide STEM consulting to the OSTP and to others, on behalf of the OSTP.

With six months to go, the senior policy advisor for STEM education at the White House Office of Science and Technology Policy had marching orders. With blind luck and good fortune to thank, hunch-based activities of the first six months had fed beautifully into meeting those objectives. No time to waste.

3

A DAY IN THE LIFE

A White House OSTP staffer who'd been there since Clinton, told me, while touring the EEOB on my sixth day, to pause and look around once in a while. Here were fossil-infused tiles beneath our feet, once trodden by Winston Churchill. There were stained-glass skylight domes over each stairway, preventively blacked out during World War II in case of bombing.

Great advice. Wish I'd followed it. The reality, though, is that everyone except for the career folks is on borrowed time and behaves like it, incessantly hurrying. This is not to say the careerists don't keep up. They do, and then some. Just imagine what it must be like for support staff in White House security, or payroll, or IT support, or scheduling, or legal, or events, or food service, or custodial, or communication, or—perhaps most challenging of all—in offices that help the administration's team interface with Congress, or the agencies, or the states, or other nations. Every four to eight years, you get a fresh crop of newbies fumbling about, tripping over rules and testing laws, earnestly pushing an agenda that might turn your stomach. Federal staffers—can I say it enough?—are unsung heroes and national treasures.

"It's easy to be consumed," said Della, my tour guide, who'd served the Clinton, Bush II, Obama, and Trump administrations. "But the people who sat in your chair five or ten years ago come back to see me all the time." She waved me into the Indian Treaty Room, the most expensive room in the whole building, for its marble wall panels and gold leaf ornamentation. No treaty had ever been signed in the room, as far as the amateur historians of the building could determine. Though, it had possibly been used to store archives, such as treaties in the early 20th century. I was agog.

"And they all say the same thing—*I wish I'd have hit pause, now and then.* You know?" She showed me some of her favorite escapes in the building—the fourth-floor library, with its window vista over the National Mall; a meditation room tucked in among the narrow halls and low ceilings of the fifth floor; and the gabled dormer window bays overlooking the White House.

Decompressing in the fourth-floor library at EEOB overlooking the south Ellipse and National Mall beyond, after the debut of America's Strategy for STEM Education

The one time I took her advice would be almost a year later—the day we dropped *America's Strategy for STEM* on the nation, amid much fanfare. After the dust settled and the dignitaries departed, I escaped to the library to breathe. Other than that, the tick-tock inside my head was too loud to let me hit pause.

While still in the negotiation phase back in fall of 2017, I took a call from Pat at the National Science Foundation, who'd been assigned to craft an Intergovernmental Personnel Act agreement to get me to DC, on behalf of the White House.

"Can you paint me a picture of what a day at work would look like at OSTP?" I said, figuring she'd helped set up those who had preceded me in past administrations.

"Well, imagine being in the position of steering national STEM policy—"

That much, I'd long since grasped. "Right, Pat, yes, that is an incredible prospect. But can you help me get granular? What does this person do on a typical day?"

I meant, what does it look like to steer national STEM policy? Is it by doing lots of solitary research and writing? Is it through working the halls of the Senate and House? Talk shows and speeches? Dealmaking over power lunches and happy hours?

"Let me put it to you this way. There're about seventy people eager to meet you," she said, as if she were telling an orphan he's about to meet new parents.

I wasn't looking to be adopted.

"So lots of meetings, then. Who're these seventy, and why are they eager?"

She chuckled, and I hoped it was over my distillation to the essence, not over my naïveté.

"Jeff, all of the federal agencies have STEM teams that carry out the directives of the administration, the Congress, and of course, our own directors and secretaries. It's the leaders of these teams, some of whom have been in this business since STEM was SMET"—an allusion to retired NSF director Rita Colwell's revision of SMET to

STEM, for its euphony in the late 1990s— "who eagerly await your arrival. As the administration's STEM guy, you'll provide them direction."

Meetings it is, then. But *seventy* would turn out to be the understatement of the year. And a *typical day* would not exist.

About a week in, a Washington lobbyist for STEM education asked me if I was "open for business." Heck, yes. I needed all the historical context and input I could get.

What happened next took almost two years to digest. But I get it now. They showed up in droves. Advocates for STEM education came from throughout the district, and from across the nation, to seek face time. Some had strong policy ideas and suggestions, while others just wanted to hear my ideas. Distinguished members of the National Academy of Sciences committees on education, and the workforce, generously met with me on several occasions to register their opinions about which policies ought to get front-burner attention, such as teacher recruitment and training. So, too, did faculty and administrators from some of the nation's most prestigious universities: *Don't forget graduate student support and research dollars.* Corporate executives came in to push for stronger workforce development emphasis in STEM education. Nonprofit executives advocated for special interests—the out-of-school community and early childhood education, to name a couple. Professional society directors argued for the centrality of their disciplines to STEM, whether it be computing, engineering, statistics, and so on. Other visitors did more listening, asking about how the policy winds were blowing in the new administration, and what that might mean for the future of STEM education.

All comers, whether listeners or tellers, studied me. They stared, sized me up, squinting over the table, cupping their ears when I spoke, nudging their next-chair neighbor now and then over something I'd not necessarily considered nudge-worthy.

It was a real déjà vu experience, taking me back to 1977, when my mother uprooted my brother and me from our high school in Iowa

City, to move us all to Massachusetts for her job. It may as well have been Marrakesh, for all we knew about New England. On my first day of class at Northampton High School, a steady stream of gawkers sidled past the open door for a glimpse of the foreigner, as if I'd come from Iceland, not Iowa. "This must be how the exotic new animal at the zoo feels," I had said at dinner that night.

The steady stream of visitors to 442 Eisenhower Executive Office Building, whether tellers or listeners, all shared a mission to discover just who on earth this administration had dug up to set a course for STEM education for years to come. Pat's guesstimate of seventy people waiting to meet me was off by an order of magnitude. By the time the dust had settled on my assignment, hundreds of meetings with thousands of STEM advocates informed my work, with typically more than three groups brought inside the wrought-iron gates daily. And they all got a glimpse of the unicorn at the zoo, setting their course for the decade ahead.

As normal a day as there was, that midsummer Wednesday. Already eighty degrees at sunrise, the city would reach a toasty ninety-three by afternoon. The president was in Brussels for NATO, and by 6:00 a.m. EST, had already made the morning news for calling Germany a "captive of Russia."

7:30 a.m.: The Navy Mess

The three-block morning walk to the Eisenhower Building, from 2020 F Street NW, challenged my antiperspirant. The coolness of the ground floor of the EEOB, with its four-and-a-half-foot-thick granite walls, awaited beyond security. Through a gate on 17th Street, flanked by Secret Service agents sporting MP5 submachine guns ever-poised for action, across a badge-activated turnstile that flashed my face on monitors lining a well-staffed security booth, place my briefcase onto an X-ray conveyor belt, go through a metal detector, and I'm in. At 7:30 a.m., the place is eerily quiet, awesomely cavernous.

Of the hundreds of people who work in the EEOB each day, two others were reliably there ahead of me every day: Della, the retired Marine who handles travel arrangements for the OSTP, and a fellow political appointee, also an Iowan, downstairs in the communications wing. They, too, avoided the daily traffic mess, by biking in from Georgetown (Della) and walking down from DuPont Circle (Iowan). The peak arrival surge is around 9:00 a.m.

On one summer morning—could've been this one—I arrived to find maintenance staff hanging giant portraits of the president and vice president in all the offices and meeting rooms. It reminded me of how leaders adorn walls in Cuba and other autocracies. Who knows, maybe all of the US presidents do this. Over time, I came to meet quite a few Obama-era staffers scattered about DC, and asked each whether they recalled giant mug shots of the president and Mr. Biden in the building during their stints. None could recall such displays.

I hurried around the workers to drop off gear at my desk and head to breakfast, a special start to the day. A senior colleague, the president's appointee to direct the OSTP, had invited me to the Navy Mess, the most elite breakfast club in America. In the basement beneath the West Wing, the executive dining hall, right next to the Situation Room, seats about fifty people, and as one might suppose by the name, it's operated by Navy culinary specialists. The table linens are embroidered with the presidential seal, and the china bears White House etchings. Oak panel lines the walls adorned with paintings of US battleships. The food is standard fare—omelets, waffles, bagels and such, though expertly prepared and served. Access to the Navy Mess is limited to Cabinet-level officials and their guests. A memorable part of it was the box of official White House M&M's handed to each diner upon exit.

9:30 a.m.: Scrum

From the Navy Mess, out the west doors of the West Wing, and up the Navy steps of the Eisenhower Building, I leaned hard into the bombproof-windowed doors, thick as a Bible, entering the first-floor hall leading to the vice president's office. Up the ornate spiral stairway—each bronze baluster of the railing individually cast—to the fourth floor, where we had a standing meeting, a scrum, every

Wednesday at 9:30. A staff of a dozen made up the technology division of the OSTP, where STEM was housed. I was old enough to be everyone's dad, including the interim director at the time—an Ivy League political science major a decade out of college, a friend of the Trumps. We assembled in a lounge at the end of our office suite, furnished with a well-worn leather couch and two matching chairs, vintage Reagan era. A flat-screen TV hung on one wall, chronically set to Fox News, on mute. A chalkboard covered the opposite wall in case of brainstorming, though typically scrawled with campaign slogan graffiti.

I'd be standing at this day's scrum, along with six others who arrived too late for a seat. Not a hardship, given their ten-minute average duration. To my right was the OSTP's congressional liaison, who'd spent most of his career as a House or Senate Republican staffer. Next, standing by the interim director, was the manager of communications, who had been recruited from the private sector, where he'd run a California marketing firm. Then came the director's assistant, an ambitious Texan who'd succeeded Bethany and aspired to someday be a policy advisor. Beside her was an intern who got a chair—a freshman at Princeton. In the other chair was an MD and academic from New York University, advising on health policy. Shoulder to shoulder on the couch were the international technology affairs advisor recruited from Google; the technology infrastructure advisor whose focus was on rural broadband access; and a cybersecurity expert on detail to the OSTP from the Department of Defense. Late arrivers standing in the doorway were a quantum expert from Harvard, and the acting director, who was heavily into autonomous vehicle policy. They were all ambitious, smart, and enormously influential in advising the president on their area of expertise. Average age in the room, with me and the intern canceling each other out, was around thirty-two.

Whatever competencies any of us may have lacked in generating national policies was buttressed by expertise across the agencies in our fields. Like me, each of them convened an interagency working group to guide them. Whenever we got a product across the finish line—whether an executive order, a presidential memorandum, or a strategic report—it was cause for fanfare on the fourth floor.

Over the course of my year on the premises, we debuted strategic plans for oceans, for addressing contaminants in drinking water, for advancing quantum information science, for cybersecurity, for medical imaging research, and for near-Earth object preparedness, to name a few. I do not recall any of it making the news. On this day, when the meeting came around to me, we were still processing feedback from a first-ever White House STEM summit a couple weeks back, to factor into a new strategic plan. For most of us, that was standard fare at scrums. We'd report: *Still working on ___ (quantum/health/5G/cyber/STEM/ etc.) ___ policy draft*. Occasional distractions and tangents arose to break the pattern, known as, *other duties as assigned*. Scrums typically ended unceremoniously after everyone reported out, with the interim director adjourning with, a timid "OK, then, good. Um...if there's nothing else, uh..."

Summoning from my distant past as a high school teacher and football coach the dismissal used for teams, I'd lean into the middle of our scrum circle, fist extended down toward eight o'clock, wondering if hands might layer on, (a few would play along), mustering "Go team!" Or to vary it, sometimes, "Ready, break!" It never fully caught on.

10:30 a.m.: Grad Students

The cyber guy and health gal followed me out, curious how they might pull off stakeholder summits similar to what we'd done for STEM. Down the hall we walked, and talked up to the threshold of a board room where fifteen graduate students in physics, engineering, computer science, and mathematics at MIT would be queued up by video to talk STEM policy.

These were members of a science communications club whose faculty sponsor had arranged this virtual meeting with me before I knew what a hassle videoconferencing would be within the Executive Office of the President. There was one laptop computer in the whole OSTP that had the capability to bypass incoming and outgoing security screening, and connect straight to the Internet. It was stored in a locked briefcase kept under close guard, very much like the so-called "nuclear football" carried by a military aide to the president whenever he travels. Using the unfettered laptop involved permissions and approvals, plus the expertise of a techie who'd configure it to a landline in that specific boardroom. Connecting to the students was a minor miracle, though still easier than getting them onto the premises.

We all introduced ourselves. They had two main interests to explore. Although I started the meeting similarly to how I had done so with hundreds of others—"What do you all believe ought to be the goals and priorities for American STEM education moving forward?"—they'd brought their own agenda.

"Actually, we'd like to begin by hearing about where the administration is heading with regard to international students—F-1 and J-1 visas, to be specific."

In 2016, more than a million international students had been enrolled in US colleges and universities, with the issuance of visas climbing for twelve straight years, until 2017, that is. I could appreciate the student's interest, and said so.

Another item they'd chosen to spend our time to explore was expressed by a Missourian pursuing her doctorate in the computational field of artificial intelligence: "Are there any plans in the works to address intellectual property theft?"

On their second question, it just so happened that I'd come to know about a division at Homeland Security working on copyright, trademark, and patent infringement. My own son had recently filed a provisional patent, and helicopter-parenting, I had quietly had coffee with the National Intellectual Property Rights Coordinator. So short answer, I offered to the MIT student, a referral to the coordinator's office.

But their first question was, unfortunately, unanswerable by me, though I'd been reading the same news that they had. In response, I paraphrased a coaching tip provided by a career staffer at the OSTP early in the gig. Otto was a deputy chief of staff whom I'd trusted enough to ask one day, in a hallway corner: "Otto, I speak with academics—teachers and professors—every day as part of this job, and they keep asking me why the president's budget keeps chopping science agencies."

He held up both hands and extended his index fingers and thumbs to form a box shape, and looked at me through the middle of it.

"You just need to stay in your box—STEM education."

I said, "Y-yeah, but—"

So Otto pressed his boxed fingers hard, pink fingernails turning white.

"People will try to take you into border control, school choice—heck, gun rights and healthcare, too. Who knows what all? Just stay in your box."

For that meeting and many encounters since, I've found respite in my STEM box.

11:30 a.m.: Media Moment

Our communications guy at the OSTP had been contacted by a reporter from a high-profile science magazine, curious about how we were coming along with the new federal STEM education strategic plan. If one were to judge by the degree of preparation for this call, it must have been of critical national importance. And I must have been in much need of media relations coaching.

In fairness to our comms guy, Rick from California, message control had come about as a tough lesson. This administration couldn't catch a break, especially in academic journals. According to Rick, they'd tussled with this particular reporter before, so guards were up. But it was a megaphone, so we'd enter into it well-rehearsed. My take, on the other hand, after a decade of media relations leading a state's STEM program, and having gotten along swimmingly with academic writers, and knowing the landscape of our topic like the back of my hand, was that minimal preparation was needed, especially from someone half my age.

Midway between Rick's and my extremes, we compromised and talked through responses to questions they'd insisted the reporter send ahead of time. Yes, I could share the emergent themes and the process we were using. No, I ought not mention any sort of timeline or hard commitments on content. And certainly no discussion of agency STEM budgets or climate change, or anything beyond STEM. I promised I'd stay in my box.

When the piece was published, plenty of liberties had been taken by the reporter, anyway, to commingle my efforts with less celebratory policy actions of the administration, such as cutting agency science budgets. Only then did I begin to have an inkling about all their fussing about media bias. But what else could they expect of a media branded "enemy of the people" by their boss?

12:15 p.m.: Broadening Participation

A legacy of the first federal STEM plan, written in 2013, were five committees chartered by the OSTP, called interagency working groups, known as IWGs. Each of them dwelt on one of the five goals of the plan—to produce more teachers, to engage informal education, to improve undergraduate retention, to make graduate education more applied, and to better serve the underrepresented. All meritorious ideas. Each IWG was populated by a dozen or two feds from across the STEM stakeholder agencies, though dominated by representatives from NSF, Department of Education, NASA, and Defense. With fewer human resources, agencies such as USDA, NOAA, EPA, USGS, Energy, Transportation, NIH, Smithsonian, and others couldn't cover all five IWGs.

One of my roles as the administration's STEM guy was to guide the IWGs, and that meant waking some of them up. By the time I got there at the start of 2018, several had been dormant since the 2016 election. Obama's OSTP crew hadn't convened them since midway through their last year in office, so it'd been about a year and a half. Meanwhile, focal areas for STEM had shifted over the past half-decade, rendering these groups due for recalibrating. I strove to attend as many of the meetings as possible, but chose to co-chair just one of them, out of personal passion.

On this day, I was convening the Broadening Participation IWG, focused on getting a greater diversity of Americans into STEM. This would be the one committee that would survive the transition from old STEM plan to new, although I'd shift the focus from four-year and graduate recruitment and retention to K-12 equity and workforce readiness. One of my favorite things to be a part of in DC, was this federal group turning the lens on itself, taking up the question of hiring within the fed enterprise. Were we drawing diverse talent? Not really. How could we change that? By approaching the Office of Personnel Management, or OPM, and changing job titles and descriptions to be more inclusive of diverse applicants.

The telephone meeting on July 11, 2018, focused on that very thing—taking up engineering as a case study. An outside group, the Institute of Electrical and Electronics Engineers, had come to brief us regarding the diverse population of Americans earning engineering technician degrees (two- and four-year credentials). If we wished to diversify the fed STEM workforce, they said, we should start by reclassifying government jobs in the engineering space so that engineering techs could apply, not just the more traditional, more theoretically (and some would say, more rigorously, yet less practically) educated engineering bachelor's and graduate degree candidates.

Well, by the time my tenure as co-chair ended in early 2019, we'd made no headway with OPM. They'd surveyed the agencies, and determined a preference for clinging to the traditional degree. I hope my successors are still fighting the good fight.

1:00 p.m.: STEM.gov

After adjourning the IWG, I rifled through the snack drawer for a granola bar, and inhaled it while descending the spiral stairs one hundred and thirty feet down to the 17th Street NW exit gate. Lunch break was a luxury few staffers indulged in unless company came through the gates. Salads munched at desks, snacks smuggled into meetings, calorie-loading breakfasts—these were common sustenance strategies. Obesity was not an issue among the staff of the Executive Office of the President. In fact, I shed about ten pounds through the 2018 tour of duty.

Dodging the ever-heavy traffic coming up 17th, I crossed to the Government Services Administration on F Street. One of the top laments I'd heard from citizens, and knew personally to be an issue with federal STEM, is how difficult it is for average Americans to find information. Grants, fellowships, camps, workshops, professional development, scholarships, and instructional materials abound across the agencies. But one could burn hours and days trying to locate opportunities. Why couldn't there be a one-stop shop, a STEM.gov, for teachers and students? Nano.gov had been launched by the National Nanotechnology Initiative. Cyber.gov had been created by the Department of Homeland Security. Health.gov had come from the Office of Disease Prevention. AI.gov had come out of the OSTP just a few months before my arrival. The interim director pointed me to the GSA to explore the possibility of STEM.gov.

I'd walked past it twice a day for a half-year, with no clue what went on inside. Its digital communications director had built AI.com. She had me step to a whiteboard and sketch out the lines, arrows, and blocks of a flow chart for how STEM.gov would work.

"Hold on." She stood and covered the last remnant of unmarked palette of white with her hands. "Well-done. I get it. We can do this. But..." She plucked the marker from my hand and gestured me toward an Aeron black netted chair of a sort ubiquitous across DC.

Arms folded, legs crossed, leaning her rump against the marker tray, careful not to lean back and erase my work onto the back of her blouse, the architect pointed out two hurdles that I would fail to clear over the remaining fifteen months on the job: the OSTP would need to pay GSA to build it, and each agency would need to commit to populating and maintaining it. Neither happened that year. Maybe my successors will see it through.

2:00 p.m.: Enlisting an Ally

For the second time in the day, I'd get to ask people what they believe ought to be the goals and priorities for American STEM education moving forward. This time, it would be the director and staff at the American Chemical Society (ACS). It was six blocks north, and one east of GSA, and I was five minutes late, and sticky under a charcoal suit complicit with mid-Atlantic humidity.

The ACS invitation, like so many others over 2018, was like a golden ticket for the access it represented—150,000 chemists nationwide. To marshal that phalanx toward a national STEM crusade would be a major advancement. What took some getting used to, though, was agenda alignment. The ACS folks, as well as the American Physical Society, the Geophysical Union, the Mathematical Association of America, the National Association of Manufacturers, the US Chamber of Commerce, and scores of other leadership groups with whom I visited through 2018, each had its own motives and interests. Naturally, everyone liked STEM education. But none opened with, *How can we help your effort?* More like, *How can the OSTP help us keep chemistry/physics/geology/mathematics/manufacturing/etc. foremost?*

It really gets to the heart of a struggle with which STEM advocates have grappled for years—a push for transdisciplinarity, or blurred lines between the disciplines, while disciplinary specialists resist being absorbed into a bigger tent. I'd do the same in their shoes. Math people love mathematics, and chemists love chemistry, and neither is keen to relinquish its specialty to a blend. Each of these meetings reinforced in my mind the importance of a *convergence* thread for a new national STEM plan that calls upon the disciplines to integrate for the benefit of learners. Silos simply won't do.

3:30 p.m.: BFFs

Back at the EEOB, I monitored my government-issued iPhone for any hitches to welcoming my 3:30 guests. The odds were maybe 10 percent that they'd stall at security and call me for help getting in.

Liam and Alicia were researchers at a think tank across Pennsylvania Avenue, called the STPI (referred to fondly as "stippy", it stands for Science and Technology Policy Institute). They'd prove to be of enormous help as contractors on the new STEM education strategic plan (my new BFFs), as they were on a number of OSTP studies, reports, and policy briefs. Frequent visitors, Liam and Alicia had successfully navigated security hundreds of times. It's the first-timers that I really had to watch. Groups could be particularly problematic, like the entire class of middle-schoolers, or the vanload of award-winning teachers I had hosted. Secret Service would have to be notified of the roster well in advance so they could all be cleared. A unique weblink to a questionnaire would come to me from security downstairs that I'd forward to the guests. Fill it out carefully, I'd advise, at least forty-eight hours before our appointment. And bring ID that matches exactly your information as entered at the link. Invariably, though, at least one, and sometimes more in any given group, would submit the form too late, or type in *Steve* when their ID said *Steven*, or mistype their birthdate or street address. All of these would stall them at the visitor entrance until I came down to verify them. And even that didn't always suffice. Many a visitor ended up sipping coffee at the Starbucks across the street, awaiting colleagues who'd gotten inside the gate with me.

The two most convincing lessons painting the inflexibility of the Secret Service had come in the previous month. First was my own mother, who came down from Massachusetts to visit. She'd completed the weblink and brought along ID, but we lingered a little too long at dinner, arriving at the visitor gate for a tour of my office around 8:00 p.m. She was denied entrance. I implored the guards, both of whom I'd become familiar with, to let this little old lady pass. No deal—her window of entrance had expired. That night, I learned the hard way that visitors had an hour on either side of the time I'd provided Secret Service to enter. Her arrival had been entered as 6:30 p.m. The only way in by 8:00 p.m. would be to find a computer and refile the security form, which, if we're lucky, would process in an hour. We walked away, committing to try again some time. But we never did.

The other incident was on the morning of the first-ever White House STEM Summit my team organized, bringing STEM leaders from across the United States, into the EEOB. Getting two hundred people cleared through the gate took a small army of colleagues and interns. But over the course of an hour, we got them all in. Dignitaries from the administration came over to make remarks. One of them—the secretary of the Smithsonian, no less—called me from the security gate about ninety minutes into the summit, his clearance window expired. He'd gotten caught up in matters at the office, then in the traffic coming over. Secret Service is an equal opportunity gatekeeper. Neither mothers nor secretaries get special treatment.

4:30 p.m.: Home Base Touch

Wolfing a bag of almonds, I skipped up the steps to the fifth-floor meditation room that Della had revealed on our tour eons ago. It was the perfect location—secure and remote—for a monthly check-in call with the team back home running the Iowa Governor's STEM Advisory Council in my absence. The topic on that particular day likely swirled around personnel, budget, policy, rules and regulations, threats and opportunities, or any combination thereof. The interim director had stepped in from industry to bridge the gap, with stellar assistance from our assistant director and program manager. All three were on the phone.

Directing Iowa STEM had been a good warmup to STEM education policy advisor at the OSTP. Similar rules, players, and politics. Just on steroids. The catch-up calls were invaluable to my resumption of the post come 2019. I had every intention of capping the DC commitment at one year, as we'd all originally agreed, notwithstanding the incessant pleas from up and down the Potomac that I extend my stay.

5:30 p.m.: National Treasures

An Obama-era OSTP staffer I'd gotten to know was now over at the American Association for the Advancement of Science (AAAS), on H Street NW. Former OSTP-ers were all over the city, actually. Some had landed at federal agencies. Others had been picked up by lobbying firms, policy institutes, and other trade or professional organizations like AAAS. So often, I'd be at a meeting or reception around the city, and up would come an earnest (they always seemed so earnest) stranger informing me, nostalgically, that she or he had been at the OSTP. Although I cherished those encounters for the collegiality, empathy, and the insights I could gain, they were always awkward. Somewhere in my onboard manual, it said to steer clear of past inhabitants of executive offices. Or maybe it was ex-officials who were bound by that rule. Either way, maybe the strain was simply the silly matter of parties, to which I did not pay much heed.

With a small number of them, I'd struck up friendships. Myron, who had worked closely on the 2013 STEM plan at the OSTP, was in charge of a new project at the AAAS, linking patent holders with schoolkids in mentorship roles—"invention ambassadors," he called them. And would I come talk to them about what's happening in STEM at the OSTP?

They were rock stars in my mind. Among them were inventors of bioadhesives to replace stitches, water purification kits for the developing world, a sensor to predict bedsores before they happen, and a colorized disinfectant that assures coverage. I gushed before these national treasures. The creativity and economic potential in that room steeled my resolve for invention education to be part of a new STEM plan. Exiting their building, I celebrated that uplifting encounter with a frozen yogurt cone.

7:00 p.m.: Brain Treat

Four blocks north and over to K Street, I arrived just in time to get a seat at the packed auditorium of the Cato Institute. The night's guest speaker was Steven Pinker, celebrated psychologist and prolific writer. His topic was a much-needed elixir—unfounded pessimism in these privileged times, based on his latest book, *Enlightenment Now*.

Of the few things I miss about DC, these public lectures rank at the top. Hearing directly from John Allen on leadership at the Brookings Institution, House Speaker Paul Ryan at the American Enterprise Institute, aquanaut Grace Young at the National Geographic Museum, and other legends opening their minds at the Worldwatch Institute, the Atlantic Council, and so on, was always a brain treat after a long day.

But sometimes a person just needs to disconnect. That's when an evening with the Nationals during baseball season, or the Wizards during basketball season, or live music at a favorite venue like Gypsy Sally's in Georgetown just about any season, scratched the itch.

8:30 p.m.: Refuge

Another wonderful thing about DC, is how densely concentrated key destinations are. Aside from occasional Metro rail trips to Alexandria or Silver Spring, my entire existence unfolded within a walkable one-and-a-half-mile radius. That was exactly the trek home to 2020 F Street NW, from the Cato Institute to end the day, jacket now slung over my shoulder, and necktie unknotted. While microwaving a tub of beans up in Studio 505, I dialed Mary. Our nightly debriefs over dinner were essential to processing and memory-banking events, both here and at home. Winding down in my swivel recliner, government-issued Dell Notebook on a lap pad, I'd tackle emails, or by July, start drafting sections of a new federal STEM plan. Eventually, the background noise of jets leaving Reagan, sirens, horns, and revelers down on the street, helicopters whizzing by, and hallway high jinks outside my door, were overridden by exhaustion. Sometimes I remembered crawling over to the bed.

Tomorrow would be just like today, except not at all.

4

CHARTING A COURSE

OSTP's lanky, spectacled chief of staff, Otto, called me into his office one frigid Tuesday morning, in January of 2018, four weeks in.

"There's quite a bit of interest in STEM on the Hill." He peered over his wire-framed glasses, forehead creased into rumble strips of flesh.

"That's fantastic," I replied, reflexively, though I was unaware of the connection to my assignment.

From my perspective, sunk into the guest chair across from him, Otto looked worried. His default.

"The agencies, especially big STEM players like NSF and ED and NASA, have to carry out any congressional edicts—"

The OSTP's congressional liaison, Sam, poked his head in the door.

"Come on in, Sam. I'm just backgrounding our new STEM guy on the landscape."

"Just today," Sam pointed at me, "the House took up a bill expanding STEM access to preschoolers."

He'd been a staffer for several House members, until plucked to translate between this administration and the Congress on all things S&T.

"Honestly," he said, "at least weekly something's introduced with a STEM component. Your arrival is timely."

I nodded, hoping somebody would tie STEM bills on the Hill to my work. Otto caught on.

Over the course of 2018, he'd reveal a sharp acuity for reading people. And he was not alone in that. A couple years later would find me in front of a roomful of undergraduate science writers-to-be, one of whom asked for the single most indelible memory I carry from my White House era. I would share that Otto and Sam, along with just about everyone at the OSTP, had remarkably high emotional intelligence, especially a sense for the minds of team members. At least, they could all read *me*—maybe I'm an open book. Or maybe people who spend years in a business, where the winning of hearts and minds based on strength of convictions, just builds a muscle for interpreting faces and postures of others.

"What Sam's getting at is," Otto said, his tone flat and frank, with what I thought was a tinge of disappointment that he had to state what, to him and Sam, was painfully obvious, "members of Congress are firing away at STEM without a target"—a typically ballistic analogy from Otto, a former naval aviator. "This administration has yet to offer guidance, a flight path."

Ah, clarity. So the strategic plan asked of me would shape what came out of Congress. Unreal.

"Sounds like we need to get cracking, gentlemen." I began to rise out of my seat.

Otto sat me back down with a raise of his palm. "It's the agencies counting on us the most on your STEM thing. This office's guidance modulates what comes out of Congress that they'll need to carry."

Otto looked at Sam, who picked up from there. "At this moment, everyone's following an expired STEM strategy of a previous administration."

My mind vacillated between, *Holy cow, it is crazy to be in this conversation,* and actually holding onto consciousness in the conversation. I suppressed the former and concentrated on the latter.

"Fellows, you have my attention," I said. "We're going to present to the agencies, to Congress"— wishing I could stand in that moment, I butt-scooched to the edge of the chair, sitting erect—"and America's entire STEM community, a plan they'll be proud of."

"Tell us what you're thinking in terms of moving forward," Otto said.

He'd been present through the 2013 STEM plan production, yet he never prescribed to, or advised me, from that experience. I took that as implied trust.

"Intake, Otto," I replied. "I'm in maximal intake mode across the agencies right now, and across the city, across all imaginable stakeholders."

So far, I'd visited two agencies and two stakeholder organizations. But I had big plans.

"And don't forget the Hill," Sam said. "I know of at least one House Science and Technology Committee chairman who'd appreciate the opportunity for input."

"Oh, certainly, Sam, I'd be honored to sit down with any congressman interested in STEM."

And then a most random question from Otto.

"How long are you thinking?"

"How long until…?" I prepared to guesstimate how long my intake process would take.

"Well, definitely we'll want to talk about your timeline sometime soon." Otto scribbled a reminder on his notepad to circle back "But for now, just tell us what you're thinking for how long the STEM plan is going to be. In pages."

One of the flaws of the first federal STEM plan in 2013, was its length. A dense, dissertation-like document, it ran 143 pages. But this was a ridiculously early moment to even ponder the length of the new one.

I stalled, scratched my chin, looked at Otto, then Sam, then Otto, then Sam, then pulled out of thin air: "Forty pages, max."

They looked at each other and chuckled.

When Bethany originally called me to say someone was needed at the OSTP to lead an update to the federal STEM strategic plan, I hid my ignorance of its existence. *There's a STEM plan?* Embarrassed, I wondered how I'd missed it. Eight years leading a state STEM program, speaking across the country on STEM, interfacing with leaders of national STEM programs and my peers at the helm in other states, writing a book on STEM education, I considered myself pretty well up to speed on the global STEM phenomenon.

Through the fall of 2017, I scrambled to learn all about the 2013 plan, titled the *Federal Science, Technology, Engineering, and Mathematics (STEM) Education Strategic Plan—A Report from the Committee on STEM Education, National Science and Technology Council, May 2013.*

Thereafter, with every colleague, before every audience, and with each correspondence, I'd ask, "Were you aware there is a federal STEM strategic plan?" The response frequency was 99 percent *no*. Exceptions occurred in some large groups, where perhaps one in five-score would raise a hand or nod. I did not test them. More universal was a reaction akin to my own—*Oh, to have known!*

Dozens of governors had initiated state STEM efforts between 2010 and 2017, and numerous corporate, philanthropic, nonprofit, and community groups had kicked off their own STEM initiatives. We all met up at annual summits conducted by US News & World Report, the National Science Teaching Association, and other gatherings to share strategies and avoid reinventing wheels. A good federal STEM plan would have saved us lots of fits and starts. We'd have been more efficient, more aligned and synchronized, more effective.

The question today is, had we known about the 2013 federal STEM plan, could it have served us that well?

The more familiar my community became with the 2013 plan, the less convinced we were that it would have been helpful in our work. It was not written for us. *Us* being STEM leaders beyond the DC Beltway. As my federal colleagues in 2018 would often remind me, that plan was speaking expressly to the agencies, providing them direction. The unfortunate disconnect in that rationale is that a STEM plan for the agencies steers how they spend the People's money through grants and programs offered to us. We were in the dark, at a disadvantage. Had we known about it, our grant proposals to the NSF, NASA, the Department of Education, the EPA, and so on, might have struck a more fundable chord. Would it have served our own STEM crusades better, as we assumed? Looking back now, I doubt it, for three reasons:

1. The plan was difficult to access. It was long and dense. Obscure "design principles" were woven into it, and it was organized around a dizzying array of categorizations, including "strategic priorities" and "coordination strategies" and "priority investment areas" and "coordination approaches" and "implementation roadmaps."

2. The plan's content strayed from community sentiment. In 2013, STEM had begun to mature into a transdisciplinary, applied, workplace-connected educational reform movement. Noble, but dated thrusts of the 2013 fed plan included emphases on producing more teachers and PhDs of singular disciplines.

3. Finally, it was unknown to exist.

By the time I arrived for the interview at the OSTP, in October of 2017, these shortcomings were clear to me. So I freely laid them out to the seven political appointees and staffers circling the table, none of whom flinched. An amply demonstrated tendency of the administration was to undo or reverse programs of the previous administration, so I supposed the idea of a complete rebuild from the 2013 plan was A-OK with them. It was not OK with the agencies, as I would come to learn.

A week after the "how long" visit with Otto in early 2018, I was back in his office to blueprint the new 2019-2023 STEM plan. This time, in addition to Sam, he'd also invited communications guy Rick. And there were two new faces, Corey and Lydia—experienced feds recruited to the OSTP in 2016. Corey had been pulled from the Management and Budget across Pennsylvania Avenue, where he was on the fast track in the information technology wing, bringing us valuable technical and leadership skills. Lydia was detailed over to the OSTP from the National Institute of Standards and Technology up in Maryland, bringing us decades of experience drafting policy reports on material science. Her chattiness belied a deep intellect.

Of the five, Otto, Sam, and Rick had been present for my descant on the shortcomings of the first fed plan at the interview months earlier, so I launched from there. The new plan has got to be more accessible to a broader audience, I insisted. Much shorter, and to the point. Simply organized around just a couple goals supported by a short collection of high priorities. For each priority, let's limit the narrative to why it's a good idea, and how to achieve it. Maybe a couple pages each. And how about sprinkling in vignettes highlighting somebody getting it right? With pictures! To round out the accessibility aspect of my brain-dump schematic, I opined that the tone ought not sound federal, but conversational. I paused. There were shrugs and nods. Keep going, Otto gestured with a swirl of his hand, and jutted chin.

Sourcing it for goals and priorities should be a comprehensive, transparent intake process, I proposed. We could be absolutely sure the content is right this time by simply asking representatives of every imaginable STEM stakeholder group their opinions, from higher education to the tech industry; K-12 teachers to nonprofits, like the Girl Scouts and museums; advocacy groups, like the Societies of Women Engineers, and of Hispanic Professional Engineers; trade organizations, like the National Association of Manufacturers, and the American Chemical Society; and—pausing for emphasis—each of the states.

Lydia flashed a you-silly-newcomer grin, and asked the other four how many people were assigned this project, and how much time was allocated to it. Nobody wanted the punchline. Otto bounced it to me. I shrugged and said I expected to enlist helpers from each of the agencies, and to knock this project out inside the year.

Rick reacted first with, "Whoo, boy."

Otto informed me that at least five OSTP members, with the help of the whole FC-STEM, had taken more than two years to produce fed STEM Plan number one. Sam leaned over and patted my shoulder sympathetically. Lydia asked Otto if she ought to make room in her portfolio for this. He wrinkled his nose, communicating, *Not now, Lydia*.

Corey, of those assembled there, the closest to the interim director, and thus particularly influential, said, "I'd bet on him," and winked at me.

Across the Potomac, the following Tuesday, for my weekly base-touch with Pat at the NSF, I sat in a lounge chair placed by her floor-to-ceiling window on the tenth floor, overlooking Old Town Alexandria, the Metro Yellow Line train clacketing by every seven minutes far below.

"That's a pretty dramatic departure," was her reaction to my blueprint for the new STEM plan.

Several of her NSF staffers had worked closely with the OSTP on Plan 1.

"Please, Pat, shoot my logic full of holes. Where're the land mines?"

Of my expanding circle of contacts across federal government, she was the most dialed in. I was grateful for her ear.

"No, the funny thing is, you make lots of sense." She gazed out the window, toward the towering Masonic National Memorial a mile west. "But it's change. People built programs and systems around the 2013 goals. There'll be friction. Resistance."

"Nothing we can't manage," I said, underestimating what lay ahead. "Propelled by the potential impact, Pat!"

"Right...about that." She focused back on me. "Your strongest pushback might be trying to do too much in one document." She was tapping the thumbs of her clasped hands in her lap. "I mean, inviting lots of outsiders into the business of the federal agencies—there's no mention of that in the COMPETES Act."

It sounded, to her, messy and uncontrolled, I suppose.

I leaned forward. "Just who do we think we are—feds—to presume to prescribe the content of a new STEM plan on behalf of the entire country?"

"And to those who will say this is a *federal* strategic plan, not a *national* one?" she said.

"I'd say it can, and should, be both."

Pat looked skeptical. The NSF would be a critical partner in the work. But if she wasn't buying, it'd likely crumble, defaulting to a touch-up of the old plan.

I said, "Nationwide input to federal writers of the 2019 plan will inform a federal product that guides federal practices that more closely align with the needs of the people served by government." I smiled. "And the odds will improve dramatically that people will like it and use it beyond I-495. Wouldn't the agencies love to have that kind of impact?"

"I think what the people at NOAA and NASA and EPA and NIH and here at NSF will say is that their first and foremost responsibility is to fulfill the mandates of the COMPETES Act, and the American Innovation and Competitiveness Act, as well as their own agency missions."

I totally understood, and started a, "Yeah, but—"

"If you want a national call to action," Pat said, "go for it. *After* completing the STEM plan."

"Pat, I don't have time to produce two major documents."

She frowned, as did everyone whenever I mentioned the one-year cap on our relationship—much too fleeting for Washington.

"Nor should there be," I said. "One federal STEM plan can steer the activities and expenditures of agencies, while also providing a unifying vision of STEM for the nation."

"You're going to have one helluva sell job rallying a federal team around generating a *unifying vision*." She said it as advice, not as foreboding.

I felt Pat was coming around.

"A new STEM strategic plan for the federal agencies that is also a rallying call to the country..." she said to the window, trying it on.

"That's it, Pat." I leaned in again. "A guiding light for STEM across the USA."

"What to call it? Maybe, a Compass for STEM."

"A lighthouse guiding STEM ships," I said, hating it soon as it left my lips.

"True North." She arched a brow. "A North Star."

"Exactly!"

I was relieved and excited. Pat was all in.

"The 2019 federal five-year plan for STEM education will also be a North Star for charting a course for STEM education throughout the nation," Pat said.

We high-fived.

Thirteen federal agencies were involved in STEM education in 2017. Each had representatives on FC-STEM, the Federal Coordination in STEM Education subcommittee, itself a spin-off of the Committee on STEM, abridged in Washington speak to CoSTEM. Both operated under the umbrella of the National Science and Technology Council in the OSTP, directed by Corey. FC-STEM members were the people Pat was thinking of who would need to be brought along on a new vision for federal STEM. I'd need them to help write it, and ultimately to approve of it and implement it. They were manager-level career employees who coordinated grants, scholarships, fellowships, camps, and professional development programs like Teacher at Sea, or Teacher in Space, among a wide variety of other STEM activities. Though they were professionally apolitical, their work lives were dramatically affected by elections, as they were about to be once more.

Over the course of the first two months of 2018, I was invited to eight of the thirteen agencies that make up FC-STEM, to meet their teams. Everyone was exceedingly kind and receptive at NASA; the Smithsonian; the USGS, within the Department of Interior; Defense;

Energy; Education; the NSF; and NOAA, within the Department of Commerce. That last meeting was held in a coffee shop across from the Eisenhower Building, unfortunately, given that their facility on Constitution Avenue is said to be spectacular. But early on, I'd received a phone call from Javier, the FC-STEM member at NOAA, who had asked to meet sooner than later.

What Javier put on the table for me was the most remarkable behind-the-scenes orientation. My only regret is that I took only minimal notes and did not record it. He'd been in this mix for three decades and readily shared recent history—views of the America COMPETES Act, honest sentiments about the first federal STEM plan, the redistribution of resources that came of it, the resultant interagency politics, and—most valuable to me—the current lay of the land as far as who was doing what across agencies. Javier cautioned me of people's uneasiness over who the election brought into their midst. He said that my qualifications in STEM were known to be fresh and strong, though my absence of federal policy background had everyone scratching their heads over what sort of advice I'd give the administration. But he judged me to be a good listener, and encouraged me to do lots more listening while getting to know the agencies. They were wildly interested in informing me about what they do.

Getting to the meetings could be a challenge for someone dependent on public transportation. The USGS in Reston, Virginia, was eighteen miles from my office. Appointments at locations radiating out from Pennsylvania Avenue generally entailed easy navigating from morning to early afternoon, when commuters were incoming or scattered across the city. But if they were mistimed to coincide with the outbound commute, plans would get jammed up.

So I accepted a 10:00 a.m. invitation to the USGS, and hopped the D.C. Metro Silver Line train from Farragut West station a block north of the White House, taking it all the way to the end of the line in Reston. From there, a city bus dropped me at Sunrise Valley Drive, and I walked up the tree-lined lane to meet two STEM leaders who were hosting hundreds of schoolkids the same day. A USGS scientist performed experimental demonstrations for them in an auditorium, and then my hosts ushered me down hallways to meet other federal geologists, chemists, and ichthyologists hard at work in their labs, each of whom had prepared activities for student groups coming by throughout the day. I'd heeded Javier's advice to speak little, such that by departure time I could recite the ample STEM portfolio of the USGS, though its FC-STEM members hadn't weighed in on my topic du jour—new directions for STEM education.

Next stop was the Defense Department's STEM operation in Alexandria, Virginia, a few days later. Known as the Mark Center, its mammoth building lay far beyond the Metro train service as well, a total of nine miles from my home base. From the Farragut West station, I boarded the southwest Blue Line bounding through a tunnel under the Potomac, and resurfacing at the Pentagon, where I exited. I joined mostly Defense workers on one of the buses that shuttle between the Pentagon and the Mark Center throughout the day. It dropped us off at the edge of a parking ramp that fed into the Mark Center.

After successfully navigating security, I was escorted deep into the center, to a boardroom where a half-dozen Defense project managers pushed brochures and flyers of their programs across the table toward me. I flipped open my portfolio, revealing a laptop that might as well have been a bomb from the way everyone recoiled and froze, pointing at the door. Oops—my host and I had neglected to stow it in a secure cabinet at the entryway. Ninety minutes later, free of electronic devices, and fully armed with Defense STEM paraphernalia, I chalked up one more FC-STEM member fully heard, though barely apprised, of changes I bring to federal STEM. Such a pattern prevailed throughout the first two months of 2018, and would bite me in March.

The United States Department of Labor was not part of FC-STEM when I arrived. Connections between the worlds of education and of work had become a hallmark of STEM education across the states as employers came to realize that their long-term talent pipeline solution was right under their noses. Tomorrow's roboticists, machinists, software developers, graphic designers, and data analysts are today's sixth graders, we in STEM pitched. Especially in the Midwest, where competing on the national stage for technical recruits is a struggle, the concept of growing your own really resonated. As a result, states like Iowa forged bonds between workforce development departments and education departments.

With that lens, I had arrived to DC, and said, "Where's Labor?"

What happened next was a one-two punch, resulting in one of my proudest legacies of the OSTP appointment.

First, the interim director of the OSTP called over to the Labor Department secretary's office and got a commitment to join. The department was thrilled to be asked, apparently. Second, during a period of multiple exploratory meetings with middle managers at Labor still dipping their toes in our water, then-Secretary of Labor Alex Acosta and I wound up at a summit lectern back to back. Offstage, I introduced myself and reinvited his department onto our FC-STEM committee, and thereby into the federal STEM strategic plan. He'd remembered and—guessing that I sensed their hesitance—reiterated the department's commitment, promising to firm up the troops. Colleagues from Labor would become premier and instrumental teammates.

The United States Department of State was also not a member of FC-STEM upon my arrival. I did not imagine that to be important until I met LaShauna, a freshly minted PhD doing a two-year fellowship at State in the field of science and technology policy. She and I both showed up at a Women in Science panel conducted at the National Academies on 5th Street NW, one afternoon during Women's History Month. Toward the end of the panel, I stood to ask the experts to explain what's behind the STEM Paradox, a curious phenomenon whereby women in developing Muslim-majority countries are much more likely to go into STEM fields than women from developed Western nations. They fumbled with it, but had no satisfactory answers.

Upon exiting the event, I was approached by two people. One was LaShauna, who said the topic had piqued her curiosity, too, since it was opportunities for women in S&T globally that had brought her to State. The other was a young staffer at the National Academies, who led both of us to a quiet corner.

"I know the answer to your question," she said, in a mild middle-Eastern accent, adding that the answer was known to every mother and daughter across Arab culture. She told us about her early years in Iran, before coming to the US for college.

Both LaShauna and I were transfixed, like she were about to reveal the Coca Cola recipe.

"From the time young girls can listen and speak," she glanced around, as if to safeguard from eavesdroppers, "their mothers constantly whisper in their ears—in Persian, of course..."

Yes, of course. We both nodded, hanging on every word.

"...'Learn well math and science, little girl, for that is your ticket to independence.'"

"Ah," we murmured, bobbing earnestly.

So that's it—we had the solution to the vexing STEM Paradox. Our Iranian friend then said something to LaShauna and me that haunts me to this day.

"So what is it that American mothers whisper in their daughters' ears?"

Over the course of several more meetings, LaShauna and I dissected what we'd heard, considering the implications. I invited her to join our development team for the new STEM plan, and she brought the US Department of State onto FC-STEM. To expand the federal interagency STEM committee by two significant additional agencies thrilled me then, and should bring great comfort to America's STEM education community for the value they add.

Federal agencies involved in STEM education populated a series of interagency working groups in 2014, to figure out how to realize the five priorities of the 2013 STEM plan. Most had been mothballed since the Obama administration's exit. Restarting these remnant committees was important for two reasons: First, they were valuable talent pools for helping to develop our new plan. And second, they could be repurposed with our new priorities. We'd just need to change their course.

Through my first two months on the job in early 2018, a total of seven IWGs sputtered to life. They convened at the Department of the chairs, at Interior just down the street from the EEOB on C Street NW, at the USDA on Independence Avenue, at NASA on E Street SW, and at NSF across the river.

One of the IWGs aimed to produce more teachers, another to improve undergraduate and graduate STEM education, yet another to broaden participation of the underrepresented. There was an IWG aiming to engage informal education, and an Evaluation IWG to figure out how to measure progress. Two others were launched afterward, independent of STEM Plan 1—a computer science working group, the CS IWG, and a Women in STEM IWG formed by advocates within agencies.

Aside from the grandeur of meetup sites, each of the IWG group agendas were similarly ninety minutes or so, with predictable rhythms—self-introductions around the table, updates on agency-specific activities in support of the IWG goal, and a welcome to the new STEM guy at the OSTP, who'll say a few words.

It was a tightrope walk to share the goals and priorities I'd brought to DC, reinforced by countless listening sessions with stakeholders and leaders, because things were trending counter to some of the work these folks had been doing. I feared the resistance of many talented and embedded federal STEM professionals. Not only could that prolong my stay, but worse yet, their pushback would dull the reach and impact of a new STEM plan. How will the teacher-production IWG react to a focus shift away from producing more single-discipline math and science teachers? Will the undergraduate-graduate IWG accept trends shifting toward skilled technical trades professions? Will the Evaluation IWG embrace an urgency to use assessment results in channeling resources? How will the CS IWG feel about emerging demand for computational literacy embedded in all coursework, versus pure computer science and coding?

I would find out how they were feeling about my agenda at the first FC-STEM meeting coming up on March 7th—my first real inkling that this would not be a cakewalk.

5

OF THE PEOPLE, BY THE PEOPLE, AND FOR THE PEOPLE OF STEM

An invitation arrived at my desk a few weeks into the OSTP. The president would be hosting the nation's governors at the White House, and one of the optional breakout sessions on workforce development needed a facilitator. It was a symbolic ask that characterized the red shift for STEM from that of the previous blue administration. I'd leveraged the political dichotomy at the state and local levels for a couple years in speeches and talks to Rotary Clubs, teachers unions, legislators, librarians, liberals, and conservatives: "There's value in STEM education, no matter which side of the aisle," I'd say of my experiences at Iowa's Capitol in Des Moines. "One side supports STEM because it's an equalizer, a moral imperative for opportunity in high-demand fields, for every learner. The other side supports STEM because it's an economic driver, a workforce development imperative for high-demand jobs." And of course, both are correct, I'd declare.

Bipartisanship is the secret to the success of the STEM education movement. Thus, a STEM education advisor of the Obama administration most probably would have, were there a governors' assembly, been asked to facilitate a K-12 education session. The new red-side-of-the-aisle administration in the White House thought of me, STEM, for the workforce development session. So in the morning of the last Monday of February 2018, I bounded down the Navy steps from the Eisenhower Building, into the West Wing of the White House, and up the stairs to the State Dining Room. Small groups of governors were assembled in the corners, chatting—no media, no assistants, just a handful of us executive office staff, security at the door, and governors.

I headed to the southwest corner, where fourteen of them waited to take up the 9:00 a.m. topic of choice with me and a young political appointee from the Domestic Policy Council, co-facilitating. Although nervous as heck and starstruck, I could not recall ever facilitating an easier group—opening with, "What are your primary workforce development challenges?" The governor of New Hampshire kicked it off, venting about the export of too many of his state's brightest minds, followed on by Alabama's governor, then Wisconsin's, Arizona's, South Dakota's, Georgia's, Iowa's, and a few others I wasn't able to identify. Fighting back the out-of-body thought wafting through my mind—*How am I here with these people, having this talk?*—I had a sudden realization.

They each cited the same challenges, in their own inimitable accents and mannerisms: a lack of entry-level skilled technical workers; a demand for increasing worker skills, too few with IT abilities; worker diversity not reflecting population diversity; brain drain to other states; an overemphasis on four-year degrees; and rural and urban employers alike, starved for applicants. And everyone also lamented the job-unready products of schools and colleges. Now and then, a governor would highlight a program of promise at a prison or a community college, or through a mosque or church.

Intimidated as I was by the group, an observation was forming in my throat that had to come out. They were missing a fundamental point that the STEM guy was duty-bound to express. The opportunity to plant a policy seed in fourteen states overrode my fear.

"May I offer the perspective," I blurted out, seizing a fleeting pause in their exchange, and raising a finger, "that your frontline workforce developers have yet to be mentioned: tomorrow's workers are today's seventh graders. Your teachers are best positioned to solve these challenges." I drained my lungs, expecting an affirmation, maybe even the launch of a new strand of discussion. Two rapid heartbeats later, Delaware's governor said the commercial fishing industry was really struggling. Louisiana's governor seconded it, leading right back into the varied job challenges to their states. Poof went my input.

We adjourned shortly thereafter. While the room got reset for welcoming the president, I chatted up a governor about his ailing Green Bay Packers, and another about her national champions, the Crimson Tide. Out of camera range, with no audience, they were just everyday folks. Tables accommodating six each were distributed throughout the room, and a lectern was placed under the watchful eye of Abraham Lincoln gazing down from over the fireplace.

I moved to a central table, occupied by the governors of Maryland, Arizona, and Indiana. The president was running late, so I distributed my business card and offered services to the governors on all things STEM education. The governor of Indiana said his state was making strong gains in STEM education, which I affirmed through the state's I-STEM program operated by a friend of mine at Purdue University. The governor of Maryland chimed in with, "Yes, so do we. We've got STEM," and might have brought up another friend of mine running his state's STEM Innovation Network, but was interrupted by a military aide at the doorway, announcing the arrival of the president.

The Q&A that followed was a stark reminder of where STEM education falls on the spectrum of priorities for governors—mid to low, depending on how successfully it aligns to workforce. School safety, however, was atop the list on this day, twelve days after Florida's Marjory Stoneman Douglas High School shooting, in which seventeen died, and seventeen more were injured. Earlier in the week, the commander in chief had tweeted "an inexpensive deterrent" to any more school shootings would be "armed educators." Several governors rose to speak passionately about the tragedy, led off by then-Governor Scott of Florida, followed by Montana's, Kentucky's, and others. Next to me, the governor of Washington rose to share with the president his view that pistol-packing teachers was a bad idea, advising that the president do less tweeting and more listening.

By afternoon, I was back out on the streets of DC, taking up invitations to visit with and hear the perspectives of STEM stakeholders. All told, I would accept 211 invitations over my first six months. Being invited to meet, as opposed to my reaching out to seek opinions, was a big deal. Word had spread virally throughout the STEM community of DC, albeit a niche fraternity, that the administration now had a STEM advisor. Otto at the OSTP had schooled me that if I were to invite anyone to advise me on federal STEM policy, then I had to invite everyone. It was a rule of the Office of Government Ethics that you can't craft federal policy based on cherry-picked input. But I could accept any of the invitations that came my way, and simply do lots of listening. That came naturally. Through January and February, some seventy-five listening-post meetings took place.

A University Opinion

Ducking into a Starbucks at the corner of Pennsylvania Avenue and 18th Street NW, I felt a cold gust blowing in behind me. The scattered patrons sipping their lattes cinched up the collars of their coats and sweaters. I winced my apology.

Already there, and rising to catch my eye from the back of the room, was the vice president of the Association of Public and Land-grant Universities (APLU). He'd brought along the manager of their STEM portfolio. I ordered a green tea and joined them. The APLU was coordinating an emergent network of STEM centers at universities across the nation, and federal direction could help or hinder its progress, depending on my advice to the administration. He knew that better than I in February of 2018. To their request for information on where the strategic planning process was leading, I simply recounted my morning with the governors—their workforce development obsession. That's an area we STEM leaders need to grow, I suggested. The VP listened intently, encouraging me to keep on blathering. His manager, on the other hand, a young recent arrival from a faculty position at an elite private college, did not suffer my chatter gladly. She corrected me freely—opining that overly focusing on workforce development would be a mistake, as would focusing on digital learning, school-business partnerships, and any other thrusts that threatened to divert resources from undergraduate and graduate science and mathematics education. I'd failed to win her confidence that we could do both. Her boss took a more productive tack, asking to circulate my contact information to leaders of a great variety of education organizations headquartered in DC, who would be eager to advise me on STEM strategic planning.

His introductions proved invaluable, each leading to additional invitations to visit with thoughtful executives—so much so that at the debut of America's Strategy for STEM Education ten months later, one of my allocated fifteen seats for guests had his name on it.

A Mathematics Opinion

Not long after my Starbucks rendezvous, numerous invitations began pouring in from higher education organizations. Of them, the most ardent were leaders of math organizations: the Mathematical Association of America (MAA), the American Mathematical Society (AMS), and the American Statistical Association (ASA). Although math was on the minds of many STEM leaders as a weak link in the STEM chain, I doubted that was behind these leaders' eagerness to meet.

Since the dawn of STEM in the 1990s—indeed, long before that—mathematics had been widely recognized as a hurdle to STEM majors and careers. Many an aspiring physician, engineer, veterinarian, chemist, and computer programmer stalled out at algebra or calculus class, diverting to prelaw or business pursuits less quantitative. And too often those who veered off have been people of subgroups underrepresented in STEM, which exacerbates inequity. Layer onto that the realization that those people driven from STEM majors because of their school mathematics grades often grow up to use numbers and calculations fluidly and effectively in their jobs and lives—we all know these people. It raises the question, *How is math being taught in school and college such that it unjustifiably weeds out diverse talent?*

That was my mindset upon exiting the 17th Street White House gate to hike eight blocks north, and arriving at the corner of 18th and Q. The headquarters for the MAA is a beautifully restored century-old five-story brick townhouse. The entire neighborhood had been torched by protesters in 1968, following Dr. Martin Luther King Jr.'s assassination. Today, the tree-lined quiet lane two blocks from DuPont Circle boasts the embassies of Montenegro, Iraq, and Botswana, alongside opulent mansions of think tanks, foundations, institutes, and museums.

The twenty-five thousand members of the MAA around the world are represented by a kind and soft-spoken director who provided me with an enchanting property tour before getting down to business. It turned out that the organization was keen to prevent a repeat of an insult that had occurred in 2012. That's when the OSTP published a report called *Engage to Excel*, calling for the production of a million new college graduates in STEM. The President's Council of Advisors on Science and Technology had penned it, recommending, among other things, that college departments other than mathematics, but which are mathematics-intensive (physics and engineering departments, for example) take over the delivery of math classes and the production of math teachers. Math people went ballistic, naturally, and rallied forces around a rebuttal paper, *Mathematicians' Central Role in Educating the STEM Workforce*, published shortly thereafter by the AMS. Surely the director was asking, in roundabout ways, *Will I centralize and not marginalize mathematics in my 2019 federal STEM plan?*

In the days and weeks to follow, my mathematics policy education continued. I answered invitations to the AMS, next door to the MAA; to the ASA, across the river in Alexandria; to the Society for Industrial and Applied Mathematics (SIAM), back downtown; and finally, to the Conference Board of the Mathematical Sciences, an umbrella group of eighteen math organizations, including each of these, along with the National Council of Teachers of Mathematics (NCTM), the Association of State Supervisors of Mathematics (ASSM), and more.

In between meetings, I enjoyed a most valued series of coffees with a retired Columbia University professor of mathematics, who directed Change the Equation, an Obama administration organization of private-sector CEOs committed to improving STEM education, especially math. She once said to me, "We keep writing the same reports over and over again [in mathematics education], but things don't change."

I'd been carrying along a paper called *Calculus for a New Century: A Pump, Not a Filter* to all of the math meetings. As its title suggests, reforming calculus class to abandon its winnowing mission was the thrust. It was published thirty years ago. I snatched it from my satchel and asked if she was familiar with the publication.

She laughed. "Exactly what I mean—that paper could've been written yesterday."

The last meeting invitation I accepted over the course of 2018 in the White House OSTP was from the Conference Board of the Mathematical Sciences, which convened on December 7th, over at the ASA in Alexandria. The STEM plan was hot off the press, and mathematics was the only singular discipline called out as a priority fix for the future. The narrative speaks to America's mathematics community in a tough-love tone, acknowledging mathematics as an essential foundation to STEM education, while commanding that math be taught better so that it filters less. In homage to the 1987 calculus paper, that section is titled "Make Mathematics a Magnet." It was received with nods of approval and gentle applause—high acclaim from a roomful of mathematicians.

Opinions of Inventors and Entrepreneurs

Innovation and entrepreneurship as priorities for American STEM education were shoo-ins, given that the America COMPETES Act reauthorization of 2010, which established a federal STEM strategic plan, also required that feds "encourage the teaching of innovation and entrepreneurship as part of STEM education activities." Now that we'd established the law of the land, the only thing left to figure out was how to interpret it for broad audiences.

Help came in the form of three particularly influential meetups. The first was breakfast with the director of the White House Initiative on Historically Black Colleges and Universities. He'd founded a nonprofit firm to uplift America's marginalized citizens through business startups, and he committed lots of his precious time to our emergent STEM plan. Though not a member of FC-STEM, the director attended every meeting and would go on to volunteer for our writing team, contributing mightily to the "Advance Innovation and Entrepreneurship Education" section. He's also to credit for at least nine mentions of HBCUs in the plan. He served as a tireless champion for his program's critical role in STEM education.

A few weeks later, the second meetup forging an innovation-entrepreneurship priority for the federal STEM plan took place at the Society for Science and the Public on N Street NW, at the invitation of the CEO. It operates some of America's premier STEM competitions, including the revered Regeneron International Science and Engineering Fair. Would I be inclined to include intellectual competitions in the new STEM plan as a means for cultivating a generation of innovators and inventors? "You bet," I replied, with a qualifier—"Let's get a greater diversity of kids into these contests." And that is how competitions made it onto page 16 of *America's Strategy for STEM Education*.

That thrust for inclusion and diversity, eventually woven throughout the federal STEM plan, was strengthened by my third encounter around innovation and entrepreneurship—this time, with a roomful of invention educators convened over at the US Patent and Trademark Office in Alexandria. Not yet having met any real inventors, I was eager to get the opinions of people who aspire to cultivate them.

The groundwork for our conversation had been laid back in December of 2017, when *The Atlantic* published "America's Lost Einsteins" by Alana Semuels. It came out on December 4th, and I had tucked a copy under my arm while boarding the plane from

Cedar Rapids to DC to begin my appointed service to the nation on December 10th. She'd digested analyses conducted by scholars about who become inventors and innovators in the USA. It detailed an alarmingly lopsided saga that handicapped our nation's innovation engine. Upon landing at Reagan National, my determination to use a federal STEM plan to push for broadening opportunities to invent had been steeled. The study concluded that if women, minorities, and people from low- and middle-income families invented at the same rate as white men from high-income families, there would be four times as many inventors in America as there are today. Too many lost Einsteins.

The *how* to developing more young Einsteins revealed itself in my meeting with the invention educators. They recognized and embraced the challenge, citing inner-city invention summer camps, maker spaces in tribal community centers, scholarships to the underrepresented for entrepreneurial majors, embedded business startup incubators in high-poverty schools, and more. As a result, innovation and entrepreneurship education, especially for America's underrepresented, is a signature priority of the federal five-year STEM strategic plan.

K–12 Opinion

Of all the stakeholders bound to be impacted by the new STEM plan, formal K–12 educators were tops on the list. If the North Star function of the document were to be fully realized, state education agencies, education support services and vendors, school district leaders, school principals, and certainly, classroom teachers would be its agents of implementation. I'm privy to that effect taking hold in states across the nation today. In Virginia, Louisiana, Nebraska, Michigan, the Dakotas, and elsewhere, programs, policies, and curricula are rolling out aligned to the priorities of *America's Strategy for STEM Education*. Most gratifying. But even if it merely reshapes how federal grants are doled out to universities and communities, what's funded must uphold goals and priorities of the federal STEM plan. That is now a reality, with grant competitions of the Department of Defense, Department of Education, National Science

Foundation, and others funding education programs that commit to bolstering content of the STEM plan. With that level of potential influence at stake, interest among educators was high when it came to offering their opinions on what should make up the content.

The US Department of Energy operates a teacher program called Albert Einstein Distinguished Educator Fellowships. Einstein Fellows are highly accomplished teachers of the STEM disciplines funded for a year in Washington to help with programs and policies in Congress and the agencies. I was excited that a dozen of them wanted to come up to the OSTP—an instant focus group to inform the new plan's direction. The conversation, were it charted, would resemble an EKG—ups and downs, peaks and valleys. I floated some exploratory priorities, and they did not hold back on honest feedback.

"It's early, but already I can predict that equity and diversity will be prominent in the plan—on everyone's minds," I said. To that revelation, I got enthusiastic nods and smiles, so I added, "...same with workforce readiness. Lots of concern that grads aren't job-ready."

Smiles drooped while blame on parents, colleges, and employers got served up.

I shifted to a universally embraced, "Nobody does not want to see STEM literacy prominent in the plan, it seems."

Amid winks and thumbs-up, someone sighed and said that it's been a goal for a long time.

"And how's that worked out?" I wish I hadn't asked. Came across as antagonistic. "Tell me what you recommend for national STEM priorities over the next five years," I said.

"More federal resources," someone replied. "Yes," a peer elaborated, "a repository or clearinghouse where all the camps, scholarships, and grants can be found."

"And fund what's proven to work," said another fellow.

"Forgivable loans for people going into STEM teaching."

"More programs like this (Einstein Fellowships) for teachers to plan, grow, and innovate."

The ideas were really bubbling.

"And how about school-business partnerships?" I said.

Umm, if we have time, sure, was the dull reception.

"And digital learning—quite a growth opportunity," I said, pre-pandemic.

In the moment though, virtual teaching and learning killed the brainstorming buzz. That sounded, to the Einstein Fellows, like a means of replacing real teachers with talking heads. Little did we all know that two years later, the entire country would fully go that route, ready or not.

As a credit to the Einstein Fellows, narrative in the new plan around the digital platforms for teaching and learning much more thoughtfully frames it as augmenting excellent teaching, not supplanting it. Their influence undergirds the overarching goals for diversity, literacy, and workforce preparation, too.

On the whole, teachers as a stakeholder group had more contributory opportunity than any other. Through spring of 2018, viewpoints of leaders from the National Science Education Leadership Association, the Computer Science Teachers Association, the National Science Teaching Association, the International Technology and Engineering Educators Association, the Association for Career and Technical Education, and many more were tallied. To top it off, 150 recipients of the Presidential Award for Excellence in Mathematics and Science Teaching took part in our first-of-its-kind Federal-State STEM Education Summit held at the White House that summer. Teachers' input weaves strongly throughout *America's Strategy for STEM Education*.

The Out-of-School Educators Opinion

Second only to the mathematics community in the earnestness of the recommendations offered was America's after-school educators. Their nationwide quest echoed my Iowa experience with professionals at our zoos, nature parks, museums, libraries, and science centers: intent on being at the table, alongside formal educators and other partners in STEM. They come equipped with undeniable statistics and other evidence of their outsized impact on learners' life paths. It turns out that many of the most distinguished scientists track back to an informal experience as their launch.

The 50 State Afterschool Network invited me to the stage of its 2018 national conference, handily in DC, so I brought along draft priorities to test on those in attendance. Politely, they applauded the emerging list, but it was during the Q&A when their light bulbs went on. I did the Q, they did the A. When hosts accord me the time, I ask for any questions, "and advice!" They had a lot to offer, not wasting the chance to weigh in on national navigation of STEM education.

"Federal agencies ought to include us in grant opportunities and partnerships alongside K–12 schools and universities," said one.

"Makes perfect sense to me," I said, scribbling on a notecard. "Next?"

"We need the same professional development that teachers do," someone else said.

"Check." I nodded. "Keep it coming."

"State education standards guide our practices, too, so we ought to be able to earn teaching credentials."

I had no doubt that was sometimes true, but stated transparently that the notion could use a task force to look at all the angles and get back to us. No one balked.

"An American child's education between 8:30 a.m. and 3:00 p.m., five days a week, ought to seamlessly integrate with her continuing education at the night sky party, the Saturday science show, and the summer coding camp."

That last suggestion translated to "Blend Successful Practices from Across the Learning Landscape," a priority of the federal STEM plan on page 13, partly inspired by the folks at the 50 State Afterschool Network conference.

The First Lady's Opinion

My boss at the OSTP, Leo, the interim director, wisely ensured that his boss in the Oval Office had plenty of opportunities for input on the emerging STEM priorities. Although I never interacted directly with the president, his daughter and his wife took increasing interest in the STEM plan as it built bandwagon momentum. In mid-February of 2018, I received an email from an assistant to the first lady, who was spearheading Melania's nascent Be Best crusade.

Early on, she focused almost entirely on kids' cybersafety from online bullying, though she later expanded to take on opioid abuse and healthy choices. Would I drop in at the East Wing to discuss our common interest?

Down the Navy steps from the EEOB, into the West Wing, where her assistant, a former campaign volunteer young enough to get carded purchasing alcohol—as was much of the staff—met me at the security desk and escorted me through the first floor hallway underneath the Oval Office, past the Red, Blue, and Green Rooms, down the East Colonnade and into the East Wing.

"Will we sit down with the first lady?" I said.

"Oh, no." My escort vigorously shook her head. "She's in New York today."

We turned a corner and stepped through the open door of a small, windowless conference room. The aide closed it and invited me to sit across the speckled ceramic tabletop from her.

"We hear from Leo that you've started putting together a new federal STEM strategy."

"Yes. And I hear from Leo that the first lady has launched her Be Best campaign. How can I help?" I pulled from my portfolio a nearly consumed yellow legal pad, with just half a blank page remaining beneath scribbles from the Einstein Fellows meeting. I dragged a heavy ink line of demarcation and scrawled *FLOTUS*.

Melania's aide, likely just a couple of years removed from phone-banking a county Republican outpost in Wisconsin, slid a stapled document across to me.

"The FTC put this together for us to help launch Be Best."

I thumbed through the brochure while she called it just a start, noting that soon many agencies would contribute content aligned to their missions. What the FTC had produced was a handbook for parents called *Talking with Kids About Being Online*. It's a coaching manual on setting guidelines, monitoring use, blocking sites or people, protecting privacy, safeguarding passwords, and advising against sexting.

"Kudos to the FTC, and to the first lady." I could not see a downside to this, whatever effect it might have, though I did not see a role for me or the OSTP. "I'm rooting for you."

"How do you think your STEM plan could help us move Be Best forward?" She'd not subtly skipped over the yes-no option to help. A White House prerogative.

"Oh, for sure, yes," I said. "It should be right that a STEM strategy for America include a call for cybersafety education."

"That's great!" Ten minutes in, and she was already checking her cell phone texts. "So send us a draft of the feature you'll include around Be Best. I'll send Leo additional content to draw from."

"OK. But months of input remain to shape the content of the new plan," I said, as the powerful millennial looked up from her phone, lips pursed. "No doubt, though, the first lady's initiative will align beautifully with our intake process," I scrambled, wholly uninterested in roadblocks or strong arms that could come from the White House.

"I am sure it will, Doctor Weld." She was out the door and down the hall before I could stow my notebook and rise. "Just take that exit straight ahead there, rather than back through the building," she called out, as I poked my head into the hall.

Through the exit outside, I skipped down a short stair, onto a walkway skirting the front lawn of the White House. It was a brisk, clear day in DC, with throngs of bundled-up tourists gazing through gate posts from Pennsylvania Avenue. In yet another pinch-me moment, I paused to consider them considering me. What I'd said on that side of the fence not so long ago: "Who's that dude, and just what the hell is he working on today?"

The walk from East Wing back to the EEOB should have taken about a minute, but I dawdled past the North Portico, taking in the moment, the lawn, the fountain, looking up at the windows of the State Floor and Residence above, the West Wing up ahead. My dream state snapped when Secret Service guards appeared over the roof rail high above, talking into collar-bone transmitters while fixed on me. Nearly breaking into a jog, I hustled to the perimeter, crossed West Executive Avenue, and darted up the Navy steps into EEOB.

The first lady's Be Best campaign earned mention on page 23 of the new STEM plan as part of a priority called Promote Digital Literacy and Cyber Safety. Though of negligible impact today, it did align with work taking place at numerous federal agencies, including the NIH, Department of Defense, the National Institute of Standards and Technology, Department of Energy, and others, as well as across states and private-sector entities that passionately advocated for cybersafety inclusion in the STEM strategic plan.

Business-Sector Opinions

Burning through yellow legal pads scrawled with the opinions of scores of advocates and stakeholders, I found consistent themes accreting. A few concretized in early 2018, thanks to particularly influential encounters. TechNet, for example, an organization representing the CEOs of America's most iconic tech firms, including Cisco, Facebook, Apple, Amazon, AT&T, and Microsoft, contributed to that effect. Leaders of the group found me on the EEOB's fourth floor to urge prominence for the *T* in STEM. All learners of all subjects, they argued, ought to be using computation in the same way that it perfuses the lives of adults at work and at play. Makes sense, I agreed, and eventually so did the writing team, building in the priority to "Make Computational Thinking an Integral Element of All Education," on page 23.

Like computation, business-school partnership was a high-frequency hope of many, ripe for concretizing, too. My audience at a US Chamber of Commerce summit of members was downright gaga over a STEM plan tilting in that direction. Focus on workforce readiness? Yes, please. More work-based learning opportunities? Amen! Connecting schools to communities and employers? Right on.

Similar sentiments sprang from the board of the National Association of Manufacturers, my audiences at the Aerospace Industries Association conference, the Institute of Electrical and Electronics Engineers, and other STEM-related employer groups that reinforced this trend. As a result, today's 2019–2023 five-year federal STEM education plan includes a goal to prepare the STEM workforce of the future, with priorities to establish educator-employer partnerships leading to community STEM ecosystems, and to expand learner work-based educational opportunities.

Three Wildcards

When former presidents of my alma mater call, I sit up straight. Three past presidents of the University of Iowa chipped in valuably to the development of priorities of the new STEM plan. One, who become the president of the American Association of Universities, conveyed an urgency for the prioritization of diversity in the STEM pipeline, which ended up as one of the overarching goals. Another became director of the Smithsonian Institution (since retired), from which he passionately advocated for the inclusion of the arts and humanities in the new STEM plan. His influence manifests in a new definition of STEM as an interdisciplinary approach to learning, with the convergence of disciplines a major priority. The third serves on the Board on Higher Education and Workforce of the National Academies of Science, Engineering, and Medicine. Her most visible contribution to the plan, making at least four distinct appearances, sprung from this advice: "Problem-solvers," she said, "are most certainly today, valuable products of STEM education. But problem-*finders*—those who can define a good question and act on it—are still quite rare."

Standard STEM coursework rarely accords that opportunity to students. As a result, *problem-finding* is now urged throughout the plan.

―――

By ten weeks into the role of STEM policy advisor for the White House OSTP, I'd accumulated from the people of STEM, a high-frequency list of priorities for the future—some new, some timeless. Every audience and encounter became a market test, the responses chronicled by my internal applause meter.

When I stopped over in Davenport, Iowa, on my way home one weekend in February 2018, members of the Quad City Engineering and Science Council willingly subjected themselves to market testing of emergent priorities for a new federal five-year STEM strategic plan.

A top-ten list was tested on each of the interagency working groups; a STEMconnector® gathering; a roomful of ecologists gathered at an Alexandria Holiday Inn; members of the National Consortium of Secondary STEM Schools; members of the STEM Education Coalition; state STEM summit attendees in Indiana and Louisiana via videoconference; countless trekkers to fourth-floor EEOB; and the Quad City Engineering and Science Council on a weekend I got back home. Through each encounter, the list was updated, refined, and strengthened, to the point where I confidently shared it with Leo and the leadership team at the OSTP, at the end of February.

"Sounds good," they said. "Proceed to share it with the FC-STEM. They need to like it."

March 7th was the first convening of the inter-agency federal coordinating committee for STEM, FC-STEM, of my tenure at the OSTP. I invited thirty STEM leaders of fifteen federal agencies up to the regal Indian Treaty Room of the EEOB. By that time, nearly each of them had seen or heard about the popular new priorities, since most were involved in IWGs, where I'd been trickling trends. This litmus test was likely to be a formality. A rally. A launch party on the writing to come. It needed to be a warm embrace, as my clock was ticking, with nine months to go.

With the OSTP leadership, and a couple of White House representatives on hand, career feds across NSF, EPA, NIH, Energy, Education, Defense, Labor, Agriculture, Homeland Security, Commerce, State, Smithsonian, Interior, Transportation, NASA, and OMB listened politely to my process, and the product that would become the backbone of a new STEM plan to steer how they all operated for the next five years – emerging new goals and priorities.

A few seconds of silence elapsed, and then the woman from USDA broke it by asking for a clarification on what is meant by the term ecosystems. Then the guy from NASA offered a tweak to digital learning. Mild approvals came from some. Others asked for time to reflect and get back to me. The tone was as good as I could have hoped.

Until...

A senior member of FC-STEM, a widely respected sage who'd served four presidents, cleared his throat.

"This would do nothing to advance STEM in my agency." He tossed the printout across the table as if it were contaminated. My lunch wanted out.

6

CHERRY BLOSSOMS AND STEMS

"If you really want to immortalize STEM during this administration..." tempted my coffee date one morning at Starbucks across from the Walter E. Washington Convention Center.

You bet I did.

He was the fourth OSTP-er from the previous administration I'd met who had worked on STEM—how luxurious it must have been to have had a team. All of them were generous with time and tips, and all had transitioned to related work in DC. He was now in charge of a massive science and engineering festival setting up in the convention center that April.

"All ears." I grinned.

My counterpart from 2016 leaned close, like so many in DC do habitually, as if divulging state secrets.

"Then you need to get it into the R&D Priorities Memorandum."

I scribbled down *R&D Policy Memo* on my legal pad, and read it back to him.

"Priorities Memorandum," he corrected. "It's an official White House document. Comes out every year." Then he furrowed his brow. "But you better hurry, unless you plan to be around a second year."

Again, the damn calendar.

"No can do." I sighed. "I bought into a one-year gig. People expect me back in Iowa for 2019."

The short window didn't bother me—with sixteen-hour workdays and no distractions, one can cover lots of ground.

"Why? What's the time frame? How do I get STEM in it?"

"You've got maybe a few weeks. The administration uses the R&D priorities to give the agencies a heads-up about what it deems to be important."

I shrugged indifference.

He raised his voice above the din of late-morning rush. "What the president expects the agencies to have in their budgets."

OK, now we're talking.

"Ah, right. That would be a legacy right up there with a new STEM plan." I gazed up through the ceiling fan, to a distant horizon.

"Bingo, Jeffrey. You'd imprint STEM on fiscal year 2019 budgets, for sure. And once it's in there, it might just stick around a while."

"Did it work for you?" I lobbed a softball. "Did you get STEM into Obama's R&D priorities?"

"Uh, yeah, big time. It's the wrap-up paragraph of a five-page R&D memo." He said it as an ex-boyfriend would—sad, but proud of the beauty he had dated and lost. And now, to me, the new boyfriend of STEM, he said, "Your team dropped the ball."

That tasted sour. *My team?* I'm solely carrying their STEM ball.

"So how's it work? Who puts it together?"

"Get with the director. Leo, right?"

"Yes...er, interim. But yes, Leo."

"Draft him something from the STEM plan you're cooking up. It'll reflect positively on his boss." Then he took a long sip on by-now lukewarm vanilla latte, and licked his lips. "It'll be the most influential two hundred words you'll ever write."

Spring was going shakily. The gut-slug that had ended the March 7th FC-STEM meeting was repeated at the April meeting by a different saboteur. Unlike in March, this was a newbie fresh from industry appointed assistant secretary in the Department of Education. In his cuff-linked and fitted suit, the former executive had arrived in Washington, gunslinging.

"I can't see anything here that my agency can rally around," he said to the FC-STEM members, not ten minutes into his first meeting.

It was three sleepless nights before I got an appointment at his sixth-floor office on Maryland Avenue SW. I employed the same strategy and got the same outcome as back on March 9th when I'd caught up with the other senior curmudgeon who'd ruined my appetite for a couple days, by blurting out a similar sentiment.

"Thanks for sitting down with me," I said. "Your indictment of a month's work in front of FC-STEM was a shocker."

"Yes, well, as I said, your goals and priorities just don't have much to do with the mission of this department." He was flanked by two young staffers who I'd come to know for their serving on STEM interagency working groups.

They'd heard, and helped shape, the backbone of the new STEM plan on numerous occasions. Both looked at me empathetically, mute.

"Sir, if you'll indulge me the opportunity, I'd like to walk through our thinking." I pulled out the top-ten list he'd dismissed, persistently optimistic.

One of my two timid advocates, eyes locked on the boss, said, "Good idea, Jeff. We could use more background."

"It's the least we can do," said the assistant secretary. "You've come all this way."

I had to believe his department was keen on equity and inclusion, I said.

"Oh, of course," he replied.

"And what about tomorrow's workforce equipped with computation and entrepreneurial skills?"

Again, strongly affirmative.

And so the pattern continued, where I simply restated what was in writing, framing each priority in the context of his building and its inhabitants. I finished the list and rested my case. His staffers winked and smiled.

"Now that you put it in that light," their boss pulled back a crisply pressed white sleeve to glance at his watch, "I'm comfortable to say we're all in."

Oh. That was bizarrely easy, after all.

The staffer who escorted me back to the front door, the one who'd spoken up to encourage the walk-through, shared that in getting to know the new boss they all learned quickly that he's a talker, not a reader, and he likes to be courted. He's not unique among this president's appointees, I'd learned since March—and I would keep on being reminded with each administration member I encountered. Each was a mental offspring of the occupant of the Oval Office.

By late April my superiors at the OSTP were getting uptight. My commitment year was one-third over, with little more to show for task number 1 than a skeletal outline. The two backfires at FC-STEM in March and April had me jittery, doubting. Also, there was the not-small task number 2 of putting to rest the 2013 plan through a final report to Congress. I was eager to get STEM into the president's R&D Priorities Memorandum; to hold a major STEM event on the South Lawn; to embed STEM into other OSTP reports percolating on quantum, oceans, manufacturing, agriculture, biotech, broadband, and 5G; and to get writing the new STEM strategic plan.

Otto, the chief of staff, ambled in to 442 EEOB one morning, as these thoughts swirled, right on cue.

"There's someone I want you to meet." He leaned on the doorframe of my office, with a leather notebook held against his chest, under folded arms—his trademark stoic leader pose. He pulled a business card out of a pocket and handed it to me. "Call this guy and set up an appointment."

I noted the address, just up Pennsylvania Avenue: the Science and Technology Policy Institute.

"What's the nature of the meeting," I asked Otto.

"These people do all sorts of jobs for us. They can help you a lot on the STEM plan. Think of them as an extra set of hands and minds. As staff."

An interesting prospect, as I was feeling overwhelmed. But what did they know about STEM? Fearing they could slow me down, I let the business card sit for days, before *they* called *me*, insistent that I come over and learn what they could do. And they bribed me with lemonade and cookies. I am so glad they did.

First mentioned in Chapter 3, The Science and Technology Policy Institute, with its acronym pronounced *stippy*, is a federally funded research and development center, one of several sprinkled across Washington, DC, each with a specialty area, such as poverty, defense, economics, and so on. STPI was established by Congress to inform and support the OSTP in particular, and other executive offices, as well as federal agencies now and then, on S&T matters. They sat me at the head of a boardroom table, surrounded by staff. Out the window, across Pennsylvania Avenue was the Gothic Eisenhower Building in its grandeur.

Although none of them claimed STEM expertise, they were physicists, engineers, technologists, and lawyers with oodles of project management experience on behalf of the White House. Assigned the STEM portfolio, if I were willing, would be Liam and Alicia, both thirty-something PhD researchers with sparkling pedigrees. They'd worked on green energy and climate change policy through Obama's OSTP, and now assisted with advanced manufacturing, space, 5G, and autonomous vehicle policy development and advice. I found them both humble, inquisitive, and brilliant. And most endearing was their fearless positivity in the face of two of the greatest hurdles I put on the table—short time frame, and pockets of resistance within key agencies.

R&D Priority Memo? Yes, they'd helped with a number of those. A closure report on the 2013 STEM plan? Similar to countless congressional briefs they'd helped to prepare for the OSTP. Embed STEM education into the various policy reports brewing across the street? Several STPI staff members were on each of those teams, so cross-pollination ought to be no problem. A major STEM event on the South Lawn? STPI had been a silent partner in planning past White House Science Fairs, so sure. Assist with launching and coordinating writing teams of feds, through summer and into fall? That was a particular strength that Liam and Alicia thought they could bring to the table—keep me focused on the big picture, while they attended to meeting logistics, calendar, and writer coordination.

That evening back at Studio 505 on F Street NW might have been my best night's sleep since arriving in DC, now that I had BFFs—best federal friends.

Not long after the engagement to STPI, Leo announced in a Monday morning scrum at the OSTP that we'd be taking two trips up to Capitol Hill that week. There was significant interest in STEM education among members of Congress, and word had spread that the White House was cooking up federal STEM policy. Leo was eager to "show off the leading STEM mind in the nation" to them. I gulped.

Our first trip, to see the House Science Committee Chair, began with a lightning-quick midmorning Uber ride of fifteen minutes from the West White House gate on 17th Street, to the Cannon House Office Building at the corner of Independence Avenue and 1st Street. The chairman of the House Committee on Science, Space and Technology—the committee that funded federal STEM programs—was a Texan who'd made no friends in the world of science, for his skepticism of climate change and disdain for basic scientific research. He'd summoned us for a briefing on how STEM policy was coming along under the young administration.

As it turned out, we were the ones briefed—I and the OSTP's congressional liaison, Sam. The congressman was a no-show. Instead, we sat with two members of his staff, both of whom had known Sam from his own days as a Republican congressional staffer. They exchanged pleasantries.

The junior staffer was a young woman who, upon my standard opener—"And tell me, did you study STEM?"—giggled nervously and said, not just no, but "Oh, no!" as in, *God, no, are you kidding?*

"Poli sci, here at Georgetown." She extended a thumb over her left shoulder, toward the northwest.

Her colleague, a bit older than I, was chief of staff. He was quick to inform us that he was set to retire right on the heels of his boss, who'd announced his congressional exit at term's end. He was gruff and smelled of cigarettes. "American history" was his answer to my opener, though he added that he's no slouch when it comes to STEM, having drafted all of the congressman's STEM legislation. I knew only of the congressman's push for more computer science in federal STEM funding and programs. Their boss the retiring House Science Committee chairman, too, was a history major and lawyer. I could only hope they listened to experts.

"Here's what we'd like to see in your strategic plan, Jeff," said the chief of staff, sitting to my right, at the table corner. He jotted on a notepad extended in my direction so we could both see his scrawling—as if we were solving a puzzle together. "Skilled trades." He underlined it, hard, three times. "The US needs technicians, man, not more PhDs."

"I think that's in line with what Jeff's been hearing. Right Jeff?" Sam wasn't really asking.

"Well, right. A skilled technical workforce is on lots of people's minds, but so are PhDs, MDs, CPAs, vet meds—"

"Americans aren't writing us a blank check," the chief said, interrupting my let's-do-it-all line of logic. "They expect us to focus on greatest needs." He scribbled while talking. "We cannot do it all." He flipped the notepad around for me to see his block letters across the top: PRIORITIZE.

"We keep hearing from the congressman's constituents," said the junior staffer, "how desperate they are for welders, machinists, installers, repairers, people who can use office software, and coders. Everything's programmed."

Based on her list, their office heard lots from manufacturers and builders, I surmised, but apparently not so much from biochemists or data analysts, finance companies, healthcare providers, or universities. This would be the trick in pulling off a national STEM plan—to please a spectrum of interests without making it a shallow, meaningless laundry list.

"Jeff, why not share some of your book?" Sam seized an opening. He'd insisted I bring a copy of my 2017 *Creating a STEM Culture*. "How did you prioritize?"

On cue, I pulled a copy from my shoulder bag and slid it across the table to the staffers.

"I'm a firm believer that a rising tide lifts all boats," I said.

It occurred to me after saying it that Red Team players might not appreciate a John F. Kennedy quote. They nodded, unfazed, or unaware.

"If we reconnect schools to communities, all career pathways open wide, locally, globally."

"You're big into business partnerships with schools." The chief thumbed through the pages. "We'd like to see more apprenticeships and internships. Less seat time in rows, listening to teachers," he growled, handing the book back to me.

I grabbed his pen and flipped to the inside cover. "And how about teacher internships with employers?" I penned a pleasantry to the congressman and his staff. "And how about students and their teachers across America working side by side with local industries on projects that serve both?" After signing in florid cursive, I handed the book back to the chief. "It's all in there, and I imagine those'll be the sorts of priorities that end up in our new STEM plan."

He rose and extended his hand. "Then I do believe that you and the congressman will get along just fine."

We promised to keep them informed of our progress. Handshakes, pats on the back, and Sam conveying hellos to assorted former Hill colleagues, if they would please, and back onto Independence Avenue we tumbled.

Days later, we returned to the Cannon House Office Building to meet with the whole House Science Committee. But this time we rode in style—an executive office black SUV driven by a Secret Service officer, arranged by Leo. I was intrigued and a little bit confused that piling in with us were Chief of Staff Otto; Rick the communications guy; Leo's personal assistant, Bethany, who was rapidly climbing from office aide to policy advisor; Sam, of course; and Corey, Director of the National Science and Technology Council. Not having known in advance that they'd all be joining us, I didn't grasp the importance of the meet-up until afterward. In hindsight, that was probably for the best. Sam had only told me that this would be a lot like our sit-down with the chairman's staff—the administration was showcasing its prized policy advisor on STEM education to the congressional committee that deals in STEM education. It would be important that they embrace the new STEM strategy, and the person behind it.

The configuration of the House Committee on Science in spring of 2018 likely lent to the amicable outcome of the meeting. Red hats outnumbered blue by twenty-one to sixteen. But in attendance were only the staff members of congressmen, a dozen or so of the thirty-seven committee members. These were senior or junior staff whose portfolios covered STEM.

We filed into a conference room where the far six chairs had been left empty. Navigating around the seated aides, Otto and Sam warmly greeted their many acquaintances. I sat and scanned the faces, trying to imagine which party each represented. A couple of them were dressed less formally—tousled hair and jeans, but nothing conclusive. Most were thirty-somethings, well-groomed and well-dressed. A middle-aged woman opposite us at the head chair welcomed everyone and invited introductions, beginning herself. Names and congressional offices for them. Names and titles for us. Me last. To my most basic, "Jeff Weld, senior policy advisor for STEM education at the Office of Science and Technology Policy," Otto piped up with augmentation. "Jeff's run Iowa's seven-year-old state STEM program for Governor Reynolds, and last year wrote the leading book on STEM." He turned from scanning them, to me. "And we're so glad he's joined the executive office to lead the administration's STEM policy work." If anyone was impressed, they didn't show it.

"Some of us were involved with the 2013 STEM plan that came out of the OSTP," said the lady at the head of the table, who was a staffer for Eddie Bernice Johnson, the ranking democrat on the committee, "and I think we'd be interested in how you might build upon it."

Exactly the place I would've started, in her shoes.

"It's really an impressive document"—which I truly believe—"and served the federal agencies well, from what I hear." That may not have been true.

"Has it served you well, Jeff, in your state leadership role?" said a young fellow two seats to the left of me, groomed like a stockbroker.

In my four months on duty at the OSTP, no one had asked how federal work had impacted my state.

"Funny you should ask." I was grateful for the opening. "Because, impressive as the 2013 plan is, I did not know it existed. None of my peers across the states knew about it." I straightened up to sell a critical new aspect—not only to these congressional aides, but to Otto and Corey, Sam and Rick. "Instead, we all invented and reinvented our own STEM strategies. It's been the Wild West. We have a chance here, with a 2019 federal STEM education strategic plan, to exponentially increase its impact by not only guiding federal agencies, but also rallying the nation's STEM enterprise around a finite set of consensus priorities."

Staffers were looking at one another, heads bobbing, lips thrust forward in a *This guy might be onto something* reaction. The OSTP gang was smiling.

"Tell us more about a set of priorities for the updated STEM plan, Jeff," said Rep. Johnson's aide, emphasizing the word *updated*.

That's how it's phrased in the America COMPETES Act—a strategic plan to be updated every five years. Fans of the 2013 plan, and of stability and consistency, had frequently reminded me of it, and would continue to do so. But the question presented me a priceless opportunity to sell the second critical new aspect for 2019.

"If you'll indulge me just a little bit of context." I reached into my satchel for a copy of *Creating a STEM Culture*, brought along again on Sam's advice. "STEM education's progressed eons since 2013. As I discuss in Chapter 1," I passed the book around, "we've become the most significant education reform movement since John Dewey. We're way past the S-T-E-M, actually. Modern STEM is about critical analysis, creative thinking, problem-solving, connecting to communities, exploring careers. It transcends the disciplines. Wouldn't you like to have experienced that kind of math or chemistry class?"

Judging by the murmured laments of school STEM experiences around the table, many congressional aides who shape science and technology law were not themselves fans of those subjects. It's a reality at every level of policy-making, from town councils to state legislatures. And it's a major problem for the advancement of STEM: the people who control it know little about it, and hated learning about it in school.

"In that context," I said, "the goals pursued by every STEM leader I know diverge from those of the 2013 plan—sometimes a little bit, and at other times significantly."

By now, my book was two-thirds the way around, getting a polite thumb-through by each staffer. Questions shifted toward the mechanical. How was I engaging the agencies in the development process? What was my timeline? Was the administration planning to back the new plan with a strong STEM budget? (Rick fielded that question: "The president strongly supports STEM, blah-blah...but we'll have to wait and see.") For my purposes, the two critical new aspects I was so hoping to deliver upon—a North Star function, and a major shift in emphasis from 2013—were alive and well in Congress.

On the limo ride back to OSTP, we chatted like chums on a road trip. I wished we could keep driving around the city for a while.

———

The media company US News & World Report has been giving STEM education a big lift every year since 2012, in conducting its US News STEM Solutions Summit. It is a premier convening of thought leaders, policymakers, industry giants, education visionaries, and communicators. It was first held in Austin, Texas, then in Dallas, Baltimore, San Diego, and a couple times—including, fortunately, 2018—in Washington, DC. I'd never missed it. When organizers phoned me in the spring of my tour of duty at the OSTP, asking me to keynote it, the allure of field-testing the nascent new goals and priorities of *America's Strategy for STEM Education* with a most savvy audience, a jury of my peers, was undeniable. The FC-STEM committee had already reacted mostly favorably to the list in March. A crowd at the US, Chamber of Commerce had received it well too. Same with the 50 State Afterschool conference, and various other small audiences. Those were warmups. This would be something of a final exam on the backbone of our 2019 strategic plan.

So when April 6th came around, I was assigned a communications deputy of Rick's, a baby-faced Texan fresh out of Southern Methodist University, where he'd majored in media studies. Together, we walked over to the convention center while he quoted inspiring passages from one of his college textbooks on how to talk to reporters. I blanked him out.

When the executive vice president for US News & World Report took the lectern, that was my prompt to slip out of the ballroom to a stage access door. Met by a handler, I was escorted to the base of the stage behind a black curtain, watching the VP from profile. He introduced me, but applause from the three hundred in attendance seemed to me tepid. Typical. Of the dozens of speaking engagements I'd accepted to that point, a familiar pattern was emerging—lukewarm reception. In fact, an occasional rise-and-walk-out that I never took personally, fully aware of people's perceptions of the administration I'd been introduced as representing. But universally—so far, anyway—we'd all ended up friendly. On many an outing, lingerers would share with me their relief over the work that someone like me was doing inside this White House. I took a deep breath, stepped to the microphone and dove in.

Ever the teacher, I invited my audience to take part in an exercise. The America COMPETES Act dictates a five-year STEM strategic plan—I framed the assignment—the first having been produced in 2013. How about a show of hands from those who have found that plan valuable? This stage-setting question always gets the same response—in a roomful of industry leaders, higher education officials, nonprofit directors, curriculum vendors, school administrators, and policy experts all gathered for their interest in STEM, not a hand went up. OK, this time it's going to be different, I promised them. Our 2019–2023 STEM plan is going to be built by, of, and for the people of STEM, starting right here.

"I have here in my hand," I waved a tattered page torn from a yellow legal pad, "a dozen goals and priorities for STEM assembled from folks like you, leaders in states, nonprofits, industry, and education."

In fact, a number of contributors were in that audience. From the lectern, I could identify a friend who operated global STEM programs for John Deere; the head of Kansas City's STEM initiative; the director of a foundation heavily investing in STEM; the founder of America's most prestigious student STEM competition; and a number of other familiar faces, including Corey from the OSTP's National Science and Technology Council, lurking in the doorway at the back of the hall.

"Let me share them with you, one by one, and give me a clap or a shout if we're on the right track."

From there, I began reciting a roster of goals not too dissimilar from what now appears in the table of contents for *America's Strategy for STEM Education*: "Diversity and inclusion in STEM?" Enthusiastic applause. "STEM workforce readiness?" Vigorous applause. "Computational thinking?" Hearty applause. "School-business partnerships?" Spirited applause. And on it went, a reception so warm and embracing that I went off the script approved by Rick and his young Texas deputy.

After thanking everyone for helping to shape federal policy on STEM, I invited anyone who had further input to call or email me, and shared my executive office phone number and White House email. Twice. Slowly, while they wrote it down. My communications assistant, alone at a table just below center stage, turned ashen, his head in his hands.

High on reactions at the US News summit, and confident that Corey had come back and briefed OSTP leadership, I approached Leo about getting STEM into the administration's FY 2020 Research and Development Priorities Memorandum. He hesitated—they already had the memo drafted and queued up for months of clearances through legal, communications, Congress, agencies, and ultimately, West Wing approval. Without STEM in it, I advised, it'll be hard to get the agencies to help with development, delaying delivery. And I rattled off the major organizations that had responded enthusiastically, especially the US Chamber of Commerce, the National Association of Manufacturers, and TechNet. "OK," he said. If I could get something to him in twenty-four hours, he'd consider including it.

My next call was to Liam and Alicia at STPI—help! We ping-ponged draft verbiage into the evening and through the next morning, until I delivered a STEM R&D priority memo to Leo at noon.

Three months later, on July 31, 2018, the White House issued its Memorandum for the Heads of Executive Departments and Agencies, which included an edited version of our memo in the section "R&D Priority Practices: Educating and Training a Workforce for the 21st Century Economy." It states:

> An American workforce capable of succeeding in the 21st century economy will require adaptability to the increasingly technical nature of work across all employment sectors and ongoing technical training. Experiential learning, such as apprenticeships, internships, jobshadows, and other employer-educator partnerships will help ensure the alignment of curriculum with workplace demands. Agencies should prioritize initiatives that reskill Americans for the jobs of today and the future. Education in science, technology, engineering, and mathematics (STEM), including computer science, will be foundational to preparing America's future workforce, and should be integrated into instruction through application to real world challenges. Agencies should work to ensure the STEM workforce includes all Americans,

including those from urban and rural areas, as well as underrepresented groups.

"If you don't want your family to remember this period as a miserable, interminable, grinding, dark episode in their lives, make them part of your adventure," said my liaison at the National Science Foundation, Pat. She, too, was on loan from a Midwestern university, winding down a three-year stint. "My husband comes out for major functions—NSF awards banquet, Independence Day parade, that sort of thing. And the dining options just cannot be matched back in Lincoln."

I'd been going home to Iowa every third weekend, but otherwise mono-focused through most of spring 2018.

"You're absolutely right, Pat," I said.

The legendary cherry blossoms of DC were fading from their peak by late April, but I coaxed my best buddy, Mary, to come out for a long weekend. The morning of her arrival, we rented bikes and toured the George Washington University campus adjacent to my apartment. Then I led the way down the Virginia Avenue hill, past the Kennedy Center, toward the Watergate Hotel, when I heard a crash behind me. Mary and a pedestrian had brushed too close, and she tumbled, splayed out on the Watergate driveway. Helpful passersby got her up and dusted her off. Her knee was bleeding, and her arm was scraped up. I sprinted sixty yards up Virginia Avenue to a CVS for bandages and ice packs, and we patched her up.

Upon her return to Iowa days later, an X-ray of Mary's elbow revealed a chip broken off her humerus. Her weekend in DC, broken arm yet unverified, consisted of finishing that bike ride, followed by a mammoth grocery shopping spree; a marathon cooking production that filled my freezer with single servings of chili, lasagna, stroganoff, stew, macaroni, and beans that would last for months; tours through the American History Museum and National Gallery of Art; an executive staff-only welcome party for the French president on the White House South Lawn; and a concert at the Warner Theatre. I think she might've popped a Tylenol now and then, but otherwise, no visible signs of suffering.

Over time, she has confessed to having had considerable discomfort throughout what I believed was one of the best weekends ever.

"There was no way I was going to wimp out. We had major things to do," she told me on the phone from back home, arm in a cast.

So many people made sacrifices and went through pains to support my mission at the OSTP—most of all, Mary. I was determined not to fail her and others with a missed target or missed deadline. The frequent and familiar click now in her right elbow is a lifetime reminder that *America's Strategy for STEM Education* was literally a joint production, a family affair.

Mary joined me in D.C. every few months for notable occasions and for blowing off steam, including the Fourth of July on the South Lawn of the White House for an executive branch barbecue, concert, and fireworks.

We were only one-third of the way there. Outwardly, I assured everyone we were right on track. We had an R&D Priority, the backing of key people in Congress, a popular consensus on goals, STPI, and the support of the interagency FC-STEM committee. Inwardly, though, I thought we had a 50-50 shot at a quality product by deadline. To write and clear a federal policy report in six months was a feat unheard of. And though I had little understanding of the process ahead, a fear gnawed at me that tidal waves of input and feedback could drown me.

7

CROSSING THE RUBICON

By midsummer, we had a solid draft of the new STEM plan when a moment arrived that I'd worried about since winter—a D-Day of sorts. The first plan, published in 2013, was peppered with quotes from and references to President Obama. From the openings of the executive summary, and the introduction to citations of his thoughts and beliefs in the director's preface and throughout, it was firmly an Obama plan. With quotes like "We don't want our kids just to be consumers of the amazing things that science generates; we want them to be producers as well," he really set the tone. For that plan at that time, it worked beautifully. But I would do everything I could to keep this president out of the 2019–2023 plan.

All the sacrifice and investment on the part of so many people would be honored only by the widest possible adoption and embrace of our new STEM plan. The payoff for all our risks and life disruptions would be squandered if this document were propped up to appear as political tripe from the administration. The people who needed it, and would use it, were academics—principally, school and college professionals—most of whom would discount it out of the gates if I let it get branded by the folks occupying the White House in 2019. Normally, I am not fond of subterfuge. But in this instance, the stakes were too high.

"We need to comb through speeches, executive orders, and presidential memorandums to get some quotes from the president about STEM," said Lydia, the seasoned editing genius the administration had brought to the OSTP from the NIST. She'd called for this meeting with just me and Corey, director of the National Science and Technology Council, who was spending more and more time alongside me on this project as Leo's observer. Lydia had printed three copies of the draft plan for the three of us to leaf through to look for insertion points for quotes.

"Has he said much about STEM?" Corey asked, glancing at me.

"Plenty." Lydia held up her hand, fingers outstretched. "He rechartered the committee on STEM, for starters." She folded down her thumb. "He invested two hundred million dollars in computer science education." Index finger. "He put STEM into the fiscal year 2020 R and D Priorities Memo." Middle finger. "Created the Council for the American Worker." Ring finger. "Executive orders expanding job training and local control of curriculum." Down went her pinky. Out of fingers, she snatched back her hand with, "Plus, a number of related actions."

"Some of that is a bit loose fitting," Corey said. Then he fell in line with his senior colleague—in age only (twice his), while maybe half his power by proximity to Leo. "We've got some mining to do, Jeff. Want to find fitting placeholders and go digging?"

"Lydia, Corey," I said, through a heavy sigh, looking eyes to eyes, back and forth, about to play my gambit. I pulled out a spiral-bound copy of the 143-page 2013 STEM plan given to me at the NSF upon arrival. Having dog-eared some pages quoting President Obama in pre-meditation, I flipped it open to them, pausing a few seconds each. "Have you seen how heavily the Obama team branded theirs?" I flipped more pages to more quotes and citations, sprinkling kerosene on their burning disdain for the previous administration. "By doing so, they unnecessarily, and probably inadvertently, politicized STEM."

"So what?" Lydia said. "Every administration does that—brands their policy reports."

Corey gave me a precious assist, as he would dozens more times in the coming months.

"What do you mean by politicizing STEM, Jeff?"

"What I mean is," I closed the spiral-bound Obama plan, and pressed both hands onto the acetate cover, "we're going to eclipse this plan by a mile. It's going to be an epic product with broad appeal—big sway on education across the country. Hell, around the globe." My eyes widened.

"And the problem with quotes is...?" Lydia was asking me, I think, though looking at Corey.

"We'd make it partisan," I said, "instantly turning off half of America. Why do that? By keeping it quoteless, we keep it unbranded by any administration and any party." And here is where I really needed Corey. "We double the impact on America's kids, teachers, communities."

"I'm seeing Jeff's point, Lydia," Corey said, coming to the rescue. "Can we minimize the quotes? The branding?" He wasn't really asking.

Lydia breathed a harrumph. "This won't clear the West Wing without mention of the president's initiatives. I will draft something."

To Corey's pained expression, Lydia added, "It'll be very discreet. But we need something in there."

And that is how there are no quotes by the administration, except for Lydia's discreet bulleted list on page 7 of *America's Strategy for STEM Education*.

Weeks before that quotes showdown, in early May, Chief of Staff Otto had summoned me to his office to lay out a schedule with milestones and checkpoints—to keep things on track. His role across the OSTP appeared to be mainly seeing to it that all trains ran on time. My philosophy was, *They hired a seasoned pro, so stay out of my hair. I'd call when I need you.* But on this particular day, a message had been sent: Attention to your little project is growing, so we need to take charge.

My first clue to the importance of this meeting was the assemblage around Otto's desk—Rick, Sam, Lydia, Corey, along with Liam and Alicia from STPI. And Leo made a rare appearance. The second clue was Leo's opening. He advised us all that this report had to be excellent; that the White House was asking about it; that there had to be unanimous buy-in across the agencies; and if I really planned to go home at the end of the year, they needed the finished product by early December. So plan accordingly.

The STEM plan's importance to the White House was validated a couple years later when, during the 2020 election campaign, the OSTP issued a report bragging on the scientific and technological accomplishments of the Trump Administration: *Advancing America's Global Leadership in Science & Technology*, featuring our STEM plan on page 33.

Leo rose, patted my shoulder, and left. As the door closed, Otto stepped to his whiteboard and uncapped a red marker.

"OK, milestones." He scribbled across the top. "Working backward from public release event on, say, December the…what's a good day? Maybe right before the holidays?"

"Friday the twenty-first?" Sam flipped through the calendar on his iPhone.

"If we could make it the tenth, a Monday," I said. "That's my last day, and I'd like to be there."

Awkward silence ensued for what seemed to be minutes, frowning faces around the table, until Otto slowly turned to the whiteboard.

"All right, December 10th it is." He wrote, pressing so hard the marker squeaked. "We wouldn't want Jeff to miss it. Then what?"

"We should do a media pre-release event," said Rick. "Get the major tech and science journals in here a few days ahead of that."

"OK, good. December 3rd or so." Otto scrawled, *Media pre-release*. "Keep going."

"You'll need CoSTEM sign-off," Lydia said. "Or maybe LRM will do. One or both, I'm not sure."

"Oh, LRM for sure on something this sweeping across agencies," said Sam.

I was apparently the only one unsure what LRM meant. It'll come clear in time, I figured.

"And all of that before the West Wing, right?" said Corey. "They should be last."

"Wait now." Otto started to jot a third milestone, but erased it with his hand and started again. "Um, let's plan on both, Lydia. So White House is last—late November. CoSTEM gives it clearance prior to that. LRM will queue up CoSTEM." He was at five milestones backed into October.

"And don't forget, you'll have the external panel in there somewhere,"said Alicia from STPI, referring to the new STEM advisory panel of citizens created by the American Innovation and Competitiveness Act of early 2017.

Final details on the makeup of that committee were still being worked out, but it would have an exclusive review opportunity.

"That's likely to be September, Otto," I said, since I'd been working closely with NASA, NOAA, NSF, and the Department of Education—the four agencies charged in the legislation for assembling the group—to populate it. "The other big milestone ahead of that will be our summit." Which was mere weeks away—a never-before-held White House STEM conference. "Oh, and FC-STEM somewhere after summit, but before CoSTEM."

Otto capped his marker without noting those last three milestones. "I'd like to ask you, Jeff, with the help of Liam and Alicia, please, to draw us up a timeline spanning now to delivery." And reading my questioning face, he added, "We'll use it to sync up every week, and sorta keep each other on course."

What a lovely offer, I wanted to think. With STPI's help, I would crystal-ball the next seven months and provide twenty-eight peeks into our journey for Otto and the leadership crew. In reality, it tasted bitter. The approach we'd undertaken was uncharted territory—intaking vast quantities of suggestions, distilling them all down to a set of goals and priorities based on frequencies and alignment to evidence, engaging dozens of writers in generating content, and editing for consistency, navigating a vetting process unfamiliar to a naïve administration, and painting a dual function for the document—federal guidance and national North Star. I did not believe time invested in atomizing our fluid process so Otto could micro-manage us was helpful.

Nor was I thirsty for more meetings. Already there were weekly scrums with the OSTP staff and the co-chairs of the FC-STEM committee, with the full FC-STEM monthly, and five operating working groups, STPI nearly daily, and writing teams just starting up, compounded by daily asks and invitations of innumerable interest groups for face time and podium time, as well as other duties as assigned.

I thus turned to STPI, my team, my assistant, my surrogate for the platoon of operatives housed in the OSTP during the Obama administration, and I asked them to produce a timeline for Otto. Given the significant dollars that the OSTP was directing to STPI for their help on the STEM plan—enough to fund a few more helpers—I had no misgivings. In fact, I asked them to coordinate the writing teams for me, too, and edit the content that came pouring in. Alicia and Liam, along with a half-dozen additional STPI professionals who got corralled into helping us on various aspects of the new STEM plan, had the perfect answer for all of my asks: *Of course. No problem. You got it.*

The STEM community across the United States is the beneficiary of that spirit, and I'm eternally grateful. Their team did an enormous amount of work.

After the program managers and deputy assistant secretaries of all the agencies and departments responsible for federal STEM approved the widely sourced and vetted new goals and priorities for a 2019–2023 STEM strategy at their April FC-STEM meeting, we set about establishing writing teams. The assignment was exceedingly difficult: in no more than two pages, present the tightest and most compelling rationale for a priority, and how the federal government will drive it. And a margin highlight box featuring a current practice in support of the priority would not hurt either. I would take on the introductory sections and closure, with the assistance of a couple NSF staffers who'd helped write the 2013 plan. With STPI's significant contributions of research support and editing prowess, we'd smooth out all of the sections farmed out to volunteers. Most of the drafting would take place in May and June, with July and August to refine and revise.

Sleepless nights leading up to this request for volunteers symptomized the absurdity of the favor asked, and the high stakes: Who among high-level federal professionals with very full plates of responsibilities at their agencies, would take on a complex chore of authoring a segment they did not choose—indeed, in some instances, did not embrace—to write a replacement STEM plan for the one that they very much liked, and that defined their current jobs? And by the way, on a tight time frame, with lots of review meetings over numerous iterations, through the heart of vacation season. No bonus pay, no relief from daily duties, and no fame or glory, though you might be included in the credits. To my amazement and relief, fifteen members of FC-STEM signed on, many bringing along colleagues, to the sum total of forty writers now listed on page ii of *America's Strategy for STEM Education*.

The US STEM community owes them all a debt of gratitude. I am eternally humbled by and fond of those folks.

But all was not easy baking. Dozens of chefs in the kitchen brought diverse opinions on key ingredients for this dish. I tussled plenty over the tone of the introductory sections, with my two co-contributors—the degree to which we ought to blaze new trails for STEM, versus merely reflect the status quo. Similarly, most of the section writing teams had some negotiating to do around key points and emphases.

The group responsible for the assessment and evaluation priorities, called Transparency and Accountability, evinced stiff resistance to the idea of common metrics to be used by all the agencies, and to the tracking of participation rates of underrepresented groups in programming. They agreed in principle, but cautioned about insufficient structures in place for capturing that data.

The group responsible for the three computational literacy priorities splintered into factions squaring off over computer science.

Microcosmic of a national debate, purists argued for computer science for all, while the more renaissance-minded favored a push for computational thinking embedded across the disciplines. The hundreds of voices I'd listened to over this priority strongly tilted toward the latter.

And the group that took on the Disciplines Converge set of priorities struggled over the mathematics priority. Why was it in there? some asked. Why was one subject area—mathematics—being singled out? others wondered. And just how prescriptive should we get in a national STEM plan in terms of telling subject area experts how to do their jobs? (the askers being mostly defensive mathematicians and math educators). But the data and research into the attractiveness of STEM and its accessibility by a greater diversity of students resoundingly implicates mathematics class as too often functioning as an unjust filter.

At every meeting of all five writing teams, I was joined by someone from STPI, Alicia or Liam, or one of their expanding stable of colleagues being drawn in to the STEM project. We fielded these and other challenging questions daily, and synchronized our coaching nightly by phone and email. I clung to the original goals and priorities of stakeholders meshed with mine and peers' experiences leading state STEM programs, in responding to and guiding writers. But in early June, two flaws in our process were surfacing. First, draft content was pouring in with writing styles all over the map. The STPI team heroically massaged reams of narrative in real time as if they had a professor of composition on retainer twenty-four hours a day. I could not keep up.

Second, and more threatening, was the editorial license taken by some of the groups to change titles and the focus of some of the priorities. A few volunteer writers seized the period of destabilization to vent concerns about the direction the plan was taking.

"Too K-12," said some. "Too postsecondary," said others. And "too workforce," came a third camp. "It needs more emphasis on teacher recruitment." "More focus on early childhood STEM." "We should have something in here about patent infringement." Among the gripes of writers, a buried friction resurfaced: "We can't make a singular document be both a federal guide and a national North Star." It was within that tenor that something interesting happened.

NSTC director Corey bounded into my office one morning of that contentious period to announce that he was "going to be all about STEM for a while." He was excited, and piled it on, stating that he was attaching to me, all up in my business, going to be my shadow, along for every meeting, every phone call. "Um, OK, sure," was my reaction, though I imagined he had plenty to do at the NSTC. Maybe he'd caught the fever—STEM was building a bandwagon.

A few days later, after the two of us had attended some writing team meetings together, I grasped his assignment. At a Transparency and Accountability committee meeting held across the street at STPI, we listened patiently to the concern of a section writer reiterating a worry that a common metric across the agencies to track and report on underrepresented participation in federal STEM programs was intractable, given the lack of data-gathering systems. Basically, heels dug in. Corey, who had surprised everyone by showing up with me, spoke to the writer's concern in this way: "It's a priority long-since approved by the OSTP and FC-STEM, and it's a high-frequency hope of the STEM community. Therefore, the administration wants us to figure out *how* to get it written into the plan, and to get past asking *why*."

Corey was the enforcer. He did the same thing a few more times at other writers meetings when questions arose regarding direction, or core content, or the North Star function of the new plan. Squeaky wheels the past few weeks had reverberated back to Leo and the leadership team, and must've gotten them worried. Go dampen the discord, Corey was likely charged. Put the administration strongly behind this. I had to sheepishly admit I needed the backup. It was a stark demonstration of how elections matter. If not for Corey flexing the political muscle of the White House, with a few antagonistic agency career professionals, they might well have undermined the project entirely. At the least, it would have been impossible to complete in a year.

Upon arrival to the OSTP in late 2017, I'd suggested we invite a few dozen of my peers from states and industry to a brainstorming session on a new STEM plan. But over the months that followed, the idea snowballed—leaders at the OSTP encouraged me to make it a national summit, a first-of-its-kind White House state-federal summit on STEM education. As much as I loved the idea, secretly I worried that, given the politically polarized times, few would come. But here's the power of STEM in America: all fifty states, and each US territory, and five Native American tribes sent representatives.

Some, in fact, overshot their quotas. With the help of the intergovernmental affairs office downstairs at the OSTP, we issued an invitation to governors of states, territories, and tribes. Each was invited to name three STEM advocates—an educator, a businessperson, and a policymaker—to come to Washington on our tab, to help set the direction for STEM. Some sent five, some sent two. A half-dozen states validated my fears by sending no one. In each of those cases, I reached out to their leading STEM advocates and coaxed them to the capital. All told, we ended up with about 190 state agency directors, state legislators, nonprofit leaders, industry executives, school chiefs, and other experts weighing in on the emergent new STEM plan while it was still malleable in June. Glorious event that it was, the summit nearly became strike two, knocking me out of mission completion.

We fouled off a curve ball thrown at our Summit in the late planning stage.

"We can't accommodate that number," said my contact at the Air and Space Museum.

We were days from welcoming a STEM crowd from across the country that exceeded our modest estimates by a third. Hosting them at Air and Space was symbolically elegant, but the strong turnout would bust their conference room.

"If you want to change to the Dulles site, then maybe," she said.

Smithsonian's much larger Steven F. Udvar-Hazy Center, at Dulles Airport in Chantilly, Virginia, is a beautiful destination for

STEM geeks, but we'd booked all guests into hotels near the White House, so the transportation logistics scared us.

"You could bring them here," came a lifeline from Aileen at the National Science Foundation, on our planning teleconference, after I rattled off all my failed phone calls for hotel ballrooms in the area, suppressing panic.

"That could just work, Jeff," said the irrepressibly positive Dylan, my co-planner for the event.

He had strolled up the stairs to my office from the Domestic Policy Council on the second floor, back in early spring, to introduce himself and ask if I needed any help. The former Eagle Scout and campaign staffer had found his DPC appointment unfulfilling, and upon hearing about STEM up in the OSTP, wanted to offer his services.

"Well, great," I'd said. We could use another researcher-writer if he was up to it.

But no, those weren't Dylan's skill sets. His fresh-from-the-fraternity appearance belied a decade's policy experience at both state and federal levels, which he cited as the skills he could offer—networking, event planning, and indefatigability. At the time, I did not see much value if he couldn't write and edit. But Dylan hung around, and in time, proved his worth ten times over.

An expert interlocutor, Dylan worked the hallways of the Eisenhower Building, bringing me priceless recon about who was rising and falling, and how ever-shifting power dynamics could affect our STEM mission. Then, when we decided on a STEM summit, Dylan's stock skyrocketed as his ability to negotiate logistics and imagine event flow came in handy. He was responsible for bringing Native American tribes into the conversation, as that had been his bailiwick while at DPC. The iconic group photo on the Navy steps was Dylan's brainstorm, too.

"Maybe," I replied, cautiously, to the NSF idea. "I mean, first, thanks for putting NSF on the table, Aileen." But I doubted that she was in position to make the offer.

A midlevel staffer, she was the executive assistant for the FC-STEM committee, and my day-to-day liaison at the foundation.

Aileen was also exceedingly detail-oriented, with access to the director. So maybe.

"I mean, I'd need to do some checking, of course," She said, reading my skepticism. "But if you're willing to seriously consider us, I'll get with facilities, security, IT, food service, transportation, and of course, the director to explore."

"We could reroute the buses easy enough." Dylan had arranged shuttles from guests' hotels to the Air and Space Museum next Tuesday morning, following our evening welcome at the OSTP Monday night. "Plus, there's always the Metro or Uber. I could put out a transportation options memo." His can-do spirit was contagious. "Some might prefer the change—closer to Reagan National for departures Tuesday night."

This relocation curveball was pitched on June 14, merely one week and a weekend from the event. By the next day, Aileen had arranged a walk-through at the National Science Foundation for me, accompanied by the heads of security, technology, facilities, parking, catering, scheduling, and other support services, all availed by request of the director. By midafternoon of Friday the 15th, we had a plan for shifting the summit to NSF. The adaptability and air of accommodation on the part of leaders at NSF, given such short notice, was among the most heartwarming spectacles I've ever seen. It helps to work at 1650 Pennsylvania Avenue.

A complication that proved to be a windfall surfaced just ahead of our historic event.

"There's another reason I want you to move the summit over here," Aileen said, at the end of our NSF facilities tour.

I had an inkling there'd been a method to her madness. I paused at the south exit door.

"We're hosting PAEMST awardees from across the country on Tuesday as well." She was referring to the Presidential Awardees for Excellence in Mathematics and Science Teaching, a White House recognition program administered by the NSF, by Aileen specifically—yet another hat she wore.

"Oh. Ugh. Really?" My shoulders slumped. "Can we all fit? Will we bump into each other? How many are coming? Can you cover both?"

"There'll be about one hundred fifty of them," she said, countering my distress with cool calm. "They'll be integrated throughout the second floor—you'll hardly notice they're here. Except..." She stepped closer to me. "Now, just hear me out, Jeff, and think about this before deciding anything."

I removed my hand from the door latch—this might last a while yet—and turned to receive her idea.

"OK, deal."

"Invite them into the summit."

"How? We're maxing out the rooms. We already have the agenda—the breakout groups. Our guests are all prepped. We...sorry, I'm not keeping our deal."

"Now you are. Thanks." She laughed. "How could the additional input of the nation's top STEM teachers be anything but good and helpful?"

It'd be a lot more work. I shrugged.

"And to them, it'd be a huge honor to help shape federal STEM policy. For you, it makes a more widely embraceable product—precious few educators are on your summit roster."

It was a major change in plans at the eleventh hour, I said. We would have to assign them to breakouts. They'd need pre-briefings. We'd need more rooms, more facilitators. We couldn't fit them into the large group sessions. And didn't they already have a full agenda?

Aileen swatted away each of my concerns like badminton shuttlecocks, having ruminated on all these challenges. She had plans in place to communicate, assign groups, recruit more staff, and connect their meeting rooms via video.

"Would you just take the weekend and consider it?" she said.

"No, I'm good." I leaned back on the exit door.

A humid June breeze rushed in. She was so convinced, and convincing. I'd grown to trust and respect Aileen as much as anyone in DC, for her intellect and professionalism.

"Let's merge the groups," I said. "This'll be a STEM plan for the ages."

She extended her hand for a high-five, and wished me a good weekend.

―――

Friends and peers, allies and legends in STEM education from across America assembled at the Eisenhower Building on the afternoon of June 25th. We held a social hour outside the beautifully restored Secretary of War Suite on the second floor. With soft drinks and angel food cake in hand, guests had the run of ten contiguous rooms first occupied by William Endicott in 1888, followed by eighteen more secretaries of war through 1939. For this and other visitor events, I had borrowed from the ornate Executive Office of the President Library on the fourth floor, Thomas Luebke's *Palace of State: The Eisenhower Executive Office Building* to read up on historic tidbits that I then dispensed on tours.

"It was likely at this very desk," I said to the four meandering delegates from the Virgin Islands—a math professor from St. Thomas, a school math director from St. Croix, the STEM manager for the territory's Education Department, and a science coordinator from St. Croix—"that Secretary of War Howard Taft, in 1908, took a phone call informing him he'd just been nominated for president at the Republican Convention in Chicago."

They politely *ahhh-ed*, and thanked me for inviting them.

Before long, we herded all guests downstairs to the auditorium, where a parade of officials was queued for welcomes. I kicked it off by reminding everyone of the significant venture they'd agreed to by showing up—helping us define the future of US STEM education. Then I introduced Interim OSTP Director Leo, followed by the president's daughter, and then a panel of dignitaries from the Smithsonian, NASA, the Department of Education, and the National Science Foundation. Then we headed for the Navy steps on Dylan's advice, to capture a group photo before sending everyone off to dinner and a good night's rest for the hard work to come on Tuesday.

Attendees to the White House State-Federal STEM Education Summit paused for a group photo on the Navy steps of the Eisenhower Building overlooking the West Wing.

Aside from the NSF director's opening remarks, a lunchtime keynote by an astronaut, and my closing acknowledgments, delegates spent the day in small table groups staffed by a facilitator and a notetaker. All had committed to pre-reading the 2013 STEM plan and our outline of goals and priorities for the 2019 plan. With twenty tables in all, along with another seven rooms of PAEMST winners channeled in via cable TV, we would enjoy a tidal wave of dozens of sets of notes advising us on how to improve on the first plan, and which of our new goals and priorities were hits and misses.

By sunset that Tuesday, after the last of our guests had scrambled to catch a plane home, my planning team circled around for a debrief. Tables were pulled together to accommodate all of us—Dylan, Aileen, Liam and Alicia of STPI; assorted interns from the OSTP and NSF; volunteers from IWGs and FC-STEM; all the notetakers from table groups; and the event's contractors from the Education Development Center. EDC, a nonprofit organization in Boston, had won the bid for NSF dollars to manage the details of this event, from booking all the flights and hotel rooms to helping plan the agenda, training the facilitators, processing all the notes, and writing up a report. The data dump consisted of pages upon pages of notes per group, amounting to roughly thirty thousand words of advice and opinion. It was a treasure trove.

In fact, it was an F5 tornado of information that presented the second existential threat to my mission after weathering disgruntled FC-STEM members earlier that spring. This time, the sheer volume of input to be processed and accommodated was overwhelming. The team from EDC said it would take them weeks, maybe months, to distill. Even then, STPI and I would need a few weeks more to package the feedback for writing groups to incorporate into their sections. If this stage in the process lasted till the harvest moon, we'd never finish by December 10th, my sworn exit.

Our embryonic national STEM plan grew in all directions at a dizzying pace after the summit. Five writing teams cranked out iterations and revisions weekly, fed raw material by me and STPI. We made what sense we could of the input from state leaders and PAEMST winners, pulling all-nighters to turn section drafts around with edits and margin notes for the writers to keep plugging away right through their own vacations and day jobs. The self-imposed rush resulted from STPI's timeline for Otto that had us presenting a draft new plan to CoSTEM by the end of July. The EDC struck a compromise to deliver what it called a bare-bones distillation of summit input on July 23, with a full report promised in four more weeks. The next day, we convened the FC-STEM group to conduct a right-hand-left-hand comparison of EDC's bare bones summary and the latest STEM plan draft, incorporating what we believed to be the main contributions of summit attendees.

Close enough was the ruling of this jury, for moving to a critical next step.

A week later, Leo and Corey convened the equivalent of a STEM Supreme Court for crossing the Rubicon with our new STEM plan—a point of no return. Members of the interagency CoSTEM are agency and department directors, deputy directors, chief administrators, undersecretaries, and assistant secretaries, listed on page *i* of *America's Strategy for STEM Education*. CoSTEM resides under the NSTC umbrella, thus Corey's lane. NSTC resides under the OSTP and Leo, who has the president's ear, so he called the meeting. But I'd be star witness. Leaving little to chance, Leo had arranged for a mock trial across the street at STPI, a couple days ahead.

"Your own passion is going to be key," said the assistant director of STPI, Carl, a laid-back former Defense Department scientist about my age, dressed like an Ivy League professor.

With an untamed mop of red hair, and thick glasses, he projected absent-mindedness. Actually, he's far from it. Of the dozen people around the boardroom table, including Corey, Liam, Alicia, and other policy analysts who'd helped out on STEM now and then, he was the only one standing. All eyes were on him.

"Your ability to sell this will make or break it," he said.

All eyes shifted to me, once again at the head of a table, on trial—an increasingly familiar, and gradually more comfortable, place with each passing day in DC.

"Sure, yes," I said. "All I can do is be honest about our product and how much the STEM community likes it."

"That's it, yes. Dwell on the process you've used to arrive at this content. They should love that." Carl had circled around to hover over my left shoulder. "And OMB..." He wagged a finger from Liam to Alicia, on my right. "You've been keeping OMB closely looped, right?"

Alicia cleared her throat and sat up straight. "Um, oh, absolutely. Someone from OMB is at every FC-STEM meeting, and I think on some writing teams, and IWGs too. Right, Jeff?"

I affirmed with a thumbs-up.

"Make sure that gets mentioned." Carl was now halfway down the table, his back to me. To the wall-length window ahead of him, he said, "OK, what else, gang?"

"Be ready to extol the improvements you're making since the 2013 plan," Corey said. "For example, what would you most want to highlight?"

I replied, "Right, er, we've built on some wonderful foundations of the 2013—"

Corey paused me with a left-handed hold-up. "Carl, correct me if I'm wrong." He upturned his hand invitingly toward the assistant director. "But wonderful or not, CoSTEM will want fresh and new, not built on, or informed by, or recycled in any way from the last administration."

"I'd say don't waste any time." Carl glanced at his watch. "This hour will be priceless real estate. And especially at first, you can capture their imaginations, or you could bore them with history."

"Copy that." I appreciated the cut-to-the-chase advice. "Along those lines, I figure they'll want to hear how their agency's been involved in development, and what they're on the hook for."

"Most definitely," said Carl. "But don't scare them with future obligations. Just the fact that their people are inner circle, having sway."

"And you might want to emphasize how STEM priorities align with the administration's other efforts," said one of Carl's analysts.

I'd seen him quite a bit up on the fourth floor of Eisenhower, where he'd been working with quantum and cyber guys at the OSTP.

"Good point. Thanks." I gave him a two-finger salute.

"And Jeff, before I have to run off here," Carl stood behind Liam, "tell CoSTEM why you're here—your qualifications, and the sacrifice you've made to do this work."

"I'll second that!" Corey said. "In fact, I'll prepare a fitting introduction for you." I was relieved not to have to toot my own horn.

"Well, listen, you've got a few minutes yet. I hope for the team here to test some more likely question on you." Carl patted Liam's shoulders. "You're in very good hands, and I know the meeting will go great."

After Carl left, the questions got more granular regarding components of the plan—the evaluation section, degrees of transparency, specific actions and investments asked of agencies, and so on. It was good, rigorous practice. At ninety minutes, we wrapped up, with Liam and Alicia offering to help me develop remarks for Monday.

"I think I got it. Thanks." I packed to walk back with Corey.

Crossing Pennsylvania Avenue to the Eisenhower, he nearly shouted in my ear amid incessant horns and sirens.

"If you win the hearts of CoSTEM, it'll be smooth sailing from here." And after another half-step, "I mean *when*."

I've not been more prepared for any meeting, nor can I recall a meeting of higher stakes for me personally and professionally, than the one with CoSTEM on July 30, 2018. Members had received our draft plan in advance, with the request from Leo to arrive prepared to approve the content and direction, or to specifically point out to us any "showstoppers."

We'd reserved Room 212 of Eisenhower, and gotten members all cleared through gate security. Known as the Diplomatic Reception Room, 212 adjoins the suite of former secretaries of state spanning 1875 to 1947. In 1898, the Spanish-American War was declared there by then-Secretary of State John Hay. On December 7, 1941, within these very walls, the Japanese ambassador to the US was dismissed by then-Secretary of State Cordell Hull upon notification of the bombing of Pearl Harbor. And the next day, Congress declared war on Japan. Our moment in history would be—understatement of the year—comparatively tame.

Following Leo's expression of appreciation for everyone's time on the part of the White House, Corey graced me with a glowing, if not, over-the-top introduction. After preliminary remarks basically restating what was in the introductory section of the STEM plan about STEM as a path to good jobs and lives for Americans, I invited CoSTEM members to comment on STEM in their shops.

The first to speak up was NOAA's deputy administrator. He brought along an iPad remotely connected to an underwater drone crawling along a seafloor out in the South Pacific at that very moment. The ten-inch screen was resplendent with tropical fish nibbling at coral, and I was transfixed, squealing to the stately assemblage, "This is what STEM is all about!"

It would go unmatched by the other agencies—no one else brought a visual aid. But USDA used a line that we in Iowa know well: Agriculture *is* STEM. And modern US food production—from seed genetics to GPS-guided tractors, to ensuring the purity and safety of the family meal—is all dependent on a strong STEM talent pipeline.

Defense followed with a similar scenario about the modern soldier as a technologist piloting unmanned aerial vehicles; programming automated weapons; and moving, seeing, listening, and communicating with augmented reality tools.

Energy cited seventeen national laboratories employing thousands of scientists across the country, all working in concert with universities and industry to advance knowledge in such diverse areas as subatomic particles, supercomputers, fusion reactors, and nanotechnology. Rest assured, we were all told, the Department of Energy depends on and expects only the best STEM education of American youth. The message from the National Institutes of Health paralleled Energy's—new drugs, new treatments, new diseases all rely on a steady stream of diverse problem solvers.

It was a common theme across EPA, Labor, and NSF—each one acknowledging a fundamental dependency on STEM education for its future. NASA's administrator saw STEM as the source of history's "stunning achievements," including men on the moon and rovers on Mars. In his honor, the term *stunning achievements* appears on pages 1 and 5 of *America's Strategy for STEM Education*.

Fittingly, the assistant secretary of the Department of Education, and the secretary of the Smithsonian, happened to occupy the two seats to my right. Having gone clockwise, they were last. The Education Department assured the room that the secretary recognized and supported the STEM education imperative, and cited several initiatives, chiefly in computer science, to bolster the nation's STEM pipeline. With the last word, the Smithsonian's secretary seized the opportunity to reinforce a call for STEM to broaden its mission, encompassing the arts and humanities as inextricable in educating creative innovators of the future. He had generously and frequently shared that view with me over the previous seven months. In his honor, the third paragraph of page 1, along with arts and humanities references on pages 15 and 20, urge Americans to broaden our definition of STEM education.

Having underestimated the time they'd each consume in proclaiming their commitments to STEM, I had just the last six minutes of the hour to deliver my presentation on how the content of the new plan was determined, how it set a new course in many respects, how their agencies had been at the table, how it all aligned with administration goals, and how I'd gotten here. It was hardly needed. Leo, seated on my left, also knew the crunch we were under, and spoke next, asking me to please use the remaining minutes specifically on agencies' involvements in input, writing, and implementation planning. That would consist of a quick rundown on the FC-STEM meetings of their subordinates, many of whom had served on writing teams and interagency working groups, too. We promised to send them each rosters to see where their people were.

With that, the clock struck 2:00 p.m. As members rose, Leo asked them if we could count on their support of the plan's draft as we moved toward finalization in the fall. There were nods, thumbs-ups, enthusiastic endorsements, and compliments of the work as they filed out. Leo and I book-ended an impromptu receiving line, thanking each member.

Corey was nagged by the prospect of agencies discounting this report upon completion. Have they really bought in, or are they just going along to get along, only to dismiss the new priorities down the road? For a young accountant riding herd at the NSTC, he had far bigger fish to fry. I was charmed by his newfound devotion to STEM.

"They absolutely cannot ignore it," Lydia said, picking up on his lament, at our weekly scrum. "Not with OMB involved."

Early on, I could not fathom a reason for representatives from the budget office being part of FC-STEM or CoSTEM. Finance fits under the *M* of STEM, I supposed. Then I met the account executive in the Office of Management and Budget, whose federal budget responsibility is science and technology—the OSTP portfolio. She told me that agencies bring forth their annual budgets for OMB clearance, and what she does is—and this, she acted out—hold up their budget in her left hand, and the administration's strategic plans in her right hand, and they have to align. If not, she sends their budget back for a rewrite. From that moment onward, I was delighted to have OMB in the room, involved in the process.

"True that," said Corey. "Just hope my bean-counter old buddies can keep agencies true to a set of hypotheticals."

"There is a more immediate safeguard if you'd like to enact it." A wry smile creased Lydia's cheek, offering a rare glimpse at her sense of humor. "We included a dot chart in the Advanced Manufacturing Strategic Plan."

Leo perked up. "You know, that is not a bad idea. Now that you mention it, Lydia, I think we should make those dot charts standard operating procedure for any interagency plan coming out of OSTP."

From the looks on faces—Dylan, Rick, Bethany, Otto—none of us had read the advanced manufacturing plan.

Dylan finally said, "Lydia, sorry, but I'm not familiar with it. What's this magical dot chart that keeps everyone honest?"

Lydia strode to the whiteboard and wiped a corner free of scribbled campaign slogans and graffiti that mysteriously reappeared daily. Likely, the interns.

"It's simply your list of goals and priorities." She drew a square and lined it into a chart. Atop the left column, she wrote *Goal*, and beneath it, 1 through 6. "And the x-axis would list the agencies committing." Across the top of each column, head tilted to write uphill, she wrote in NSF, DOE, EPA, NOAA, NASA, USDA, DOD, and then ran out of room for anymore.

"Would this dot chart be internal only?" I said, skeptical that agencies would publicly commit to goals and priorities.

"That is the point," said Lydia. "As presented, it's just a dot. Innocent and easy."

Leo picked up the thread. "Serious peer pressure kicks in when agencies come in strong and weak with their dots. Over the course of a week, more and more dots."

As much as I hated the idea of shaming agencies into proclaiming their commitments to goals and priorities of the STEM plan with dots, it turned out to work surprisingly well. Early on, agencies such as USDA and Commerce, came in strong with their dots, while others dragged their feet. Eventually, the chart got filled in, with most agencies committing to multiple priorities, as depicted on page vii of *America's Strategy for STEM Education*.

It was enormously gratifying to know that our work would have a lasting legacy on the practices and investments of fifteen federal agencies and departments for years to come. If, that is, we could pull off the greatest feat of them all—clear the labyrinth that lay ahead, requiring unanimous consent. Or die.

8

OTHER DUTIES AS ASSIGNED

Annual White House science fairs had become legendary across the US STEM community, with wide media coverage of President Obama interacting with bright young Americans who invent, model, and solve through science, mathematics, and technology. The fairs were held for seven years, from 2010 to 2016. And in 2014, they introduced a White House Maker Faire, too, along with math and engineering design student recognitions, all coordinated by staff at the OSTP. There had been hints coming out of the White House for openness to a possible 2017 science fair on the South Lawn, but it never materialized.

"Why don't we organize a White House STEM festival?" I asked Leo and the team, at our weekly scrum, early in my appointment.

Back home in Iowa, we ran countless STEM fairs, and had it down pat. An event crew would be required, though, and the ranks were thin at the OSTP compared with the Obama years. If we enlisted help from the Domestic Policy Council and the West Wing, it could be a reasonable task with big media coverage.

"Let me run that up the flagpole at the White House." Leo scanned his notepad for the next agenda item.

Weeks went by, and it became the second-most asked question of STEM-ers I hosted or visited on my rounds. Right after asking what would be in the new STEM plan, they'd say, "Hey, will you be continuing the White House science fairs?" And I'd take it back to a scrum and get an "Oh, right, yes. Still checking," from Leo. It appeared that this administration did not grasp or appreciate the power of such an event—the positive optic and warm glow it could cast. But an Oval Office dealing in 2018 with constant staff turnover, shutdowns, school shootings, Stormy Daniels, Michael Cohen, John Bolton, Omarosa, James Mattis, Rex Tillerson, Jeff Sessions, Andrew McCabe, the Mueller investigation, and myriad other crises would likely dismiss a request for a STEM event like an annoying gnat.

Then one day in February, Leo stuck his head in my office doorway.

"Ivanka wants to see what you have in mind for a STEM fair."

It was the first register of interest, and a reveal of whom in the West Wing would be our STEM liaison. I would see much more of Ivanka in the months to come.

"On it!" I was excited to modernize the event, elevating STEM education as the logical successor to a typical layer-cake school experience—math class, computer class, science class. Using a White House showcase to inspire systemic change toward transdisciplinary, community-based learning would be a proud legacy.

Thus, days later, I presented to Leo a two-page prospectus for a White House School-Business Partnerships Showcase. It'd be held in late spring or early fall, on the South Lawn. Governors would nominate exemplary community partnerships between schools and employers guided by a check-off list of qualities, including career coaching, classwork linked to real workplace challenges, and diverse profiles of student participants. The Office of Intergovernmental Affairs would communicate with states. The White House Visitor Center, Photo Office, Management and Administration Office, Personnel Office, Digital Strategy Office, Communications Office, Facilities Management Navy Mess, and Secret Service each had roles ranging from transportation, publicity, and logistics to meals, displays, and security. The FC-STEM committee would be the selection panel to choose the twenty-five or so projects to be showcased. The president would peruse and celebrate the partnerships on display, encouraging more of this across the nation. It aligned perfectly with the administration's agenda, and would model the best in STEM education for the nation.

Leo must have done his part to move the concept up the chain, because shortly thereafter, I took a call from Ivanka's chief of staff, inviting me to come discuss it in her West Wing office. The former Goldman Sachs executive told me that Ivanka was interested in the twist on science fairs, a critical shift to highlighting workforce development-related education. It was something the administration could get behind, she said, and promised to get back to me soon.

Disappointingly, I never heard back on that. They never pulled the trigger in the West Wing. Thank goodness, in hindsight—it would have sucked precious time from more impactful chores to come, likely delaying my exit.

A big time-sink became the G-7 and G-20 international summits. The forty-fourth summit of the global G-7 nations took place in June of 2018, and STEM was part of the agenda. I was surprised and thrilled to be invited by Andrei, the OSTP's senior advisor on international technology matters, to help him prepare. He sat two offices north of me, but was rarely in. And when he was, Leo was with him, or he was in Leo's office, the two of them young, handsome, plotting, powerful peas in a pod, whispering, perking up and freezing like a pair of prairie dogs when threats (anyone) appeared at the door.

"What do you need?" one or the other would say.

Both were in their mid-thirties. Leo's West Coast suburban upbringing and Ivy League pedigree contrasted with Andrei's Romanian childhood and Oregon adoption in middle school. His accent persisted, particularly in words containing a *th*, so *the* became *duh,* and *that* was *dat,* and *throw* was *trow. Jeff* was *Zhaiff.* Andrei had been a whiz kid with computers, and landed at Apple out of college, rapidly rising through the ranks before packing up for Washington on Leo's invitation to join the OSTP. Now, here were these two young gentlemen, weeks from representing the USA around a table of their counterparts from Canada, France, Germany, Italy, Japan, and the United Kingdom. Of course I'd help.

The G-7 meeting in Quebec would focus on gender equality and jobs of the future, according to the advance materials flooding my email inbox from Andrei. Beginning around Valentine's Day, and continuing through March, frequent telephone calls were arranged by the Canadian prime minister's sherpa, a guy tasked with refining the official agenda through pre-debates with advisors across the member nations. Each of these calls was preceded by urgent, twenty-four-hour-turnaround requests from Andrei. Could I please summarize the status of American women in tech fields? How about a dozen talking points, please, around the best practices for drawing diverse talent into STEM careers? Would I please review and mark up iteration number X of a draft declaration of commitment to lifelong learning that members would be asked to sign?

By the time we sent Leo and Andrei out the door for the G-7 summit, they were loaded up like kids heading for camp. Instead of snacks, swimsuits, and comic books, their satchels were full of three-ring binders of harvested wisdom from advisors upon which they'd advance the human condition. Of the twenty-eight commitments that came out of the summit, as *The Charlevoix G7 Summit Communique*, one was familiar to me, as I'd worked it over a dozen times:

> 8. We are resolved to ensure that all workers have access to the skills and education necessary to adapt and prosper in the new world of work brought by innovation through emerging technologies. We will promote innovation through a culture of lifelong learning among current and future generations of workers. We will expand market-driven training and education, particularly for girls and women in the science, technology, engineering and mathematics (STEM) fields. We recognize the need to remove barriers to women's leadership and equal opportunity

to participate in all aspects of the labor market, including by eliminating violence, discrimination and harassment within and beyond the workplace. We will explore innovative new approaches to apprenticeship and vocational learning, as well as opportunities to engage employers and improve access to workplace training.

I was never briefed on how the meeting went. Nothing was reported out at our scrum. There was a mysterious cloak of silence. According to media reports, the president had pushed hard for Russia to be included (G-8), to no avail. He had apparently insulted Prime Minister Abe of Japan, as well as Canadian Prime Minister Trudeau. France dubbed the event "G6+1," portraying the US as outside the sandbox. Ah well, at least Andrei had been well-prepared.

A *Groundhog Day*-esque repeat of this process and sequence occurred again in the fall, when Andrei prepared to accompany the administration to the bigger G-20 summit in Argentina. Once again, jobs of the future were on the agenda. The outcome document, the *G20 Leaders' Declaration* of thirty-one commitments included several focused on STEM education that reflected our input— vocational training and skills development, including reskilling workers, bridging the digital gender divide, and increasing women's participation in STEM and high-tech sectors. So, success.

But as with the G-7 summit, our contributions were overshadowed by the administration's mis-steps. For example the U.S. team made the decision to pull out of the Paris climate accord, which they chose to reiterate as item 21 of the *Leaders' Declaration*. Item 20 immediately preceding the US pullout was a restatement from the other nineteen nations to full and irreversible commitments to the Paris Agreement. G19+1?

There were two offices that could, with a phone call, blanch cheeks of political appointees and career staffers alike: The Office of Management and Budget, and the Government Accountability

Office. The first document plopped on my new desk upon arrival at the OSTP in December of 2017, was a report from the GAO, courtesy of Chief of Staff Otto, my first occupant of the guest's chair.

"There's never going to be a good time to spring this on you, so let's get it over with." He exhaled and leaned back.

I thumbed through the paper, a report to Congress titled *Managing for Results—GAO-16-509*. Full of acronyms and fed-speak, it mentioned STEM on every couple pages, but the upshot wasn't jumping out at me.

"That sounds ominous, Otto. What do we have here?"

"What we have..." He stroked his chin with rounded fingertips nearly vacant of gnawed nails, and curled his lower lip inward so that the next thing he said probably was *is*, but sounded like *eeaawwhs*.

What the hell. Out with it.

"I'm on it, Otto. Whatever." I risked sounding like a hayseed optimist, but I'd put out innumerable policy fires at the state level.

"This is one of the two main reasons we need a STEM lead at OSTP," he said, finding an angle to proceed. And he began to spill. "We just haven't told you about it. Fulfilling the congressional mandate for a new STEM plan is task one, of course. But close on its heels is cleaning up a mess left by the first STEM plan."

"Why is anything to do with a 2013 report the problem of this administration?" I said, irritation hatching deep within my brain.

I cherished the visioning and future focus of the mission they'd sold in getting me here. Any minute spent fixing a shortcoming of a soon-to-be-irrelevant policy of my predecessors would be a distraction, retrograde, a bureaucratic burn-off.

"STEM education was named a CAP goal—a Cross-Agency Priority—by the Obama administration in 2015..."

The way that Otto emphasized *Obama* prompted my mind to wander. What must it have been like for him to oversee the sea change at OSTP in 2016? Adieu to brilliant legends John Holdren and Megan Smith. Hello to a scant troop of bright but unproven unknowns bolstered by expertise borrowed from the agencies.

Focus.

"...and once that happened, the GAO kicked in to audit progress toward the CAP goal on behalf of Congress. Whoever's president when their audit comes out, inherits any problems."

"Why don't you, or Leo, call over to GAO and let them know that we're about to replace the plan that's fallen short"—slim odds, I knew, but needed a glimpse into the power dynamic between the executive branch and GAO—"and say, this time we'll get it right?"

Otto removed his glasses to rub his eyes. I thought his patience was shortening.

"You will definitely press the reset button upon delivering the new STEM plan, Jeff. But until then, we need to answer with remedies."

Or else? I never verbalized the question, nor did it ever get answered over the course of dealing with the GAO. All I know is that every document exchange between me and GAO was proofread and critiqued by the whole leadership team—legal counsel, congressional liaison, NSTC director, communications, chief of staff, and interim director. And sometimes agency directors, too, if they were mentioned. A leash was kept tight on me in any dealings with GAO—I couldn't phone them without permission.

"How bad is it?" I said. Perhaps some of the objectives of Plan 1 hadn't been reached, and there was little I could do about it. "What's the process from here?"

"Mostly data-gathering promises made and not kept," said Otto. "Evaluation and efficiency stuff. Read through it and start thinking how you'd recommend we address the gaps."

Considering that assessment in the 2013 plan was entirely the responsibility of the agencies, I was initially skeptical that I or the OSTP could do much. That was before I knew the power of our positions with the agencies.

Otto continued. "Seven different CAP goals are included in this report, so it's just a skim of shortcomings. In a few weeks, they'll issue a STEM-specific report with firm recommendations that we *must* act on. You'll be our lead." Otto popped up and clapped once. "Great to have you on board." And off he went.

True enough, a couple weeks later, we received an internal draft of the STEM-specific report for comment before its public release in mid-March. The official report, *STEM Education: Actions Needed to Better Assess the Federal Investment, GAO-18-290*, stirred up a tizzy at the OSTP and within the major STEM agencies, including NSF, NASA, the Department of Education, NOAA, and Energy. It was as if they'd gotten an F on their report card. For me, it commenced almost weekly phone calls—closely monitored—with the two examiners at GAO who'd written the report. They detailed the shortcomings for me and coached a process ahead, entailing quarterly reports on progress ameliorating the failings. Those failings, summarily, were:

1. There was no annual progress report to Congress regarding STEM in 2017, a failed responsibility of the OSTP working with the interagency CoSTEM.

2. Fewer than half of the 163 federal STEM programs across 15 agencies had produced evaluative data specific to a requirement of the America COMPETES Act—to track and report the participation rates of women, underrepresented minorities, and persons in rural areas in federal STEM programs.

3. Overall performance of STEM programs across federal agencies was not collected by the OSTP and CoSTEM. Thus, they could not use the information to identify complementary, as well as redundant, programs for making annual adjustments (also a directive of the COMPETES Act).

My first high-profile duty at the OSTP was to lead the administration's response letter to the draft report to be included as an appendix upon its public release. Our "Yeah, but..." rejoinder. It was a high-wire balancing act to acknowledge the shortcomings I agreed with, while pushing back on behalf of agencies held liable.

That letter, a product of dozens of meetings and countless iterations reviewed by CoSTEM, FC-STEM, and the OSTP leaders, appears as Appendix IV on page 37 of the GAO report. The balance might best be captured by this statement on page 2:

We have reviewed the [recommendations], and with expanded capacity now in place at the OSTP to support CoSTEM, we will move forward to put processes and strategies in place to consider how to address each one in a meaningful way over the coming months.

In other words, I got this.

Each quarterly report to GAO from there detailed the progress we were making in building an audit-proof 2019–2023 STEM plan. Today, the new STEM plan answers the GAO with five priorities moving forward, on pages 28–33 of *America's Strategy for STEM*. They may well be the most potent parts of the entire work:

- Leverage and scale evidence-based practices across STEM communities.
- Report participation rates of underrepresented groups.
- Use common metrics to measure progress.
- Make program performance outcomes publicly available.
- Develop a federal implementation plan and track progress.

"What should we be doing to prepare to maybe someday work here?" was one of the best questions asked of me, by a guest to the fourth floor of the Eisenhower Building, all year.

The inquirer was a Hoboken seventh grader, one of the thirty national finalists of the Broadcom MASTERS competition—some of the brightest kids in the country. By this measure, anyway. I was thrilled to host them for the insights they might provide for the emerging STEM plan. They would probably have preferred a White House science fair, but I was their consolation prize.

"Keep doing just what you're doing." Unimaginative, so I pressed on. "Keep striving. Stay curious." Then I editorialized: "Hang around with positive people, and be nice to everybody." Trending toward lecture: "Thank your teachers and parents all the time. And be humble." Their eyes began to glaze over, so I hastened to flip it. "OK, your turn. Help me with a new national STEM education plan. What should we do so all kids can have the opportunities you're having?"

Their responses validated their selection as smarties.

"Well, not everybody has computers and Fitbits and things like that to do research," said a fidgety girl, her peers nodding emphatically.

OK, check. You're right in line with our overarching thrust toward equity, diversity, and inclusion.

"Great. What else?"

A hand went up at the end of the table—a dapper young fellow with a booming voice.

"Um, what I like about the MASTERS is that we get to work on real problems instead of, like, just theories or memorizing."

His handler, the DC-based director of the program, sitting a few feet behind him, smiled broadly, likely because he'd nailed a tenet of her program.

MASTERS is an acronym for Math, Applied Science, Technology, and Engineering for Rising Stars. And I smiled because the 2019 STEM plan was going to strongly push connections between learning and life beyond school, at work and in communities.

They were astoundingly prescient about the direction our new plan was heading. Advice ranged from blending classes so that they connect more (Check: our transdisciplinary learning priority); more freedom to create and invent, instead of using cookbook lab manuals (Check: our innovation and entrepreneurship priority); more emphasis on how to think, and less on facts (Check: our STEM literacy goal); and more. Though our meeting lasted only an hour, that group of middle schoolers did more to shape *America's Strategy for STEM Education* than most other groups I met with—partly by honing the content, but also by billowing my sails during equatorial doldrums of momentum.

Other youthful voices contributing to our North Star for American STEM education included high school Chief Science Officers (CSOs), scholars from the World Food Prize, and the previously mentioned graduate students at the Massachusetts Institute of Technology.

Twenty-two CSOs from across the nation—elected by their peers to advance STEM education in their schools and communities—descended upon Washington for a crash course in federal science and technology policy. I was grateful they wanted to come up to the OSTP for a confab. Their mark on the federal STEM strategic plan is on page 34, a section now titled "Using This Plan." The high school CSOs took their roles as advocates quite seriously. Their responses to my invitation to help shape a new national plan for STEM education centered on actions they could take to help amplify the document's impact. Rather than offer suggestions for content, they ideated a section of the plan that implores readers to advocate. They inspired the clarion call that concludes *America's Strategy for STEM Education*.

The World Food Prize scholars and MIT graduate students were latecomers to my leased commitment to the feds. I welcomed both groups into the Eisenhower Building (virtually for MIT) in early fall of 2018, when policy was solidifying. The World Food Prize, based in my home state of Iowa, awards collegiate scholarships for agriculture-related majors focused on global food challenges. The scholars expressed their passionate commitments to safe, equitable, and sustainable farming and food production practices worldwide. Our conversation became a Kumbaya of shared hopes for STEM education, as a means toward that end.

The graduate students at MIT were studying science policy and communication, and similarly chose to use our time together to share their STEM policy passions. One was patent infringement—several recent lawsuits were cited by a computer major who was obviously well-informed in setting up her question. Qualcomm had successfully sued Apple for using its battery-saving chip in iPhones without permission. A small e-cigarette maker shared its vape pod design with the RJ Reynolds company in hopes of investment or partnership, only to have the design allegedly ripped off by the tobacco megacompany. And Hanes, the underwear maker, sued Jockey for copying Hanes's sports bra design. Finally, she asked what I and the OSTP were doing about intellectual property theft. Good question. Next?

Their other topic of interest was international student and scholar visas. I guessed that several of the students were at MIT on F-1 student visas and knew faculty who were there on the J-1 visas issued for instructors. Did I support the president's recent restrictions on both types of visas, and would there be further or fewer restrictions ahead? Fascinating topics, I acknowledged, but both beyond my purview. Stay in my box.

One hour of progress on federal STEM lost—the middle school kids had been more insightful. I'd connect them to experts in those arenas, I promised, drawing the meeting to abrupt closure.

"Bring the STEM guy," I overheard the president's director of strategic initiatives call over his shoulder to my colleague Franco, as their band of technophiles breezed by my office one day. He'd spotted me in the doorway of 442 Eisenhower, and waved emphatically, mouthing, *Come on. Come!*, while keeping step with the fast-moving swarm.

Franco had come into the OSTP on the same day as I—December 11, 2017. He'd driven down from Cambridge, where he was a professor in both physics and computing, a marriage he'd orchestrated to drive the frontier of knowledge in quantum information theory.

He was cheery and kinetic—we'd hit it off instantly. Our first rite was an interminable orientation at the hands of a career office administrator who plodded through a notebook of laminated sheets detailing locations of various services in the building—post office, tech support, cafeteria, health station, etc.—all in monotone. I teased our acclimator with questions like, "Which offices, in sequence, would I visit first to last to be most efficient, to save time?" Franco joined in, requesting that she map on a legal pad he'd handed her, the location of restrooms and stairways so that he could plot his bathroom breaks. The staffer played right along, snapping out of zombie mode, and we all had the best, nerdiest of orientations in quite some time, I would guess.

Franco was brilliant, I came to learn—not through him. He was modest and kind. But our bios were circulated to the entire team upon hire, and Franco's included the highest of honors, awards, patents, and recognitions, for piercing the shroud of fundamental challenges to realizing and understanding quantum coherent devices—which, by the way, use subatomic energy units such as electrons or photons in ultracold containers to store information.

Quantum computing is still borderline science fiction, but Franco leads the charge, and he was hand-picked by the strategic initiatives director, whose trademark pace had the pack moving at near jogging speed. A former executive for an auto manufacturer in Detroit and a major tech firm in Silicon Valley, the director had been brought on as the president's utility player, trolling the halls of the OSTP for the next big thing. Artificial intelligence, powered by quantum, was in his crosshairs. I hustled to catch up and join them.

Being the OSTP's "STEM guy" meant I'd be invited to many such meetings. Franco and the quantum-AI team were the first of a dozen that year to couple grand aspirations for future global dominance in a science or technology arena with preparing a fertile garden of talent, starting—they recommended—at the level of community colleges.

"Too late," I meekly interjected, at that first meeting.

Franco said to please continue.

"The quantum talent pipeline, like every other STEM pathway, is at this moment a trickle of mostly male, mostly white, mostly suburban and affluent candidates. The competition for them at the college level is fierce. Why not reach back further, into K-12, and help swell the pipeline? More for you. More for engineering and actuary, and every other college major currently competing for the few."

At their second meeting, I was asked how they could get more American teachers trained to teach about quantum, even as early as elementary school. Grateful to have shifted their thinking, I hesitated to layer on another peccadillo when it came to industry engaging with schools. What the heck, I decided—stakes are high, and my time is short.

"This field of inquiry is inherently interesting to youth and teachers, no doubt," I began my sermon, repeated with nanobiotechnology, advanced manufacturing, 5G, autonomous vehicles, space leadership, ocean economics, semiconductors, energy systems, and other study groups that year. "But to focus exclusively on developing lessons and training for quantum education, you'll inevitably compete for precious classroom time with the biotech, or energy, or environment, or health, or Internet of Things, or robotics, or cybersafety camps, each of which might act in a silo of self-advancement. Teachers across the country would be confused by the cacophony, picking and choosing, or maybe throwing up their hands." Finally, my oft-repeated sermon concluded. "If we work across the disciplines and specialties to help teachers and kids to own foundational skills and understandings in computing [or energy systems, ecology, cells, communications networks, statistics, depending on the group I was addressing], using your pioneering advancements as captivating examples, we'd have an educational tide that'd lift all boats."

As I did whenever I gave this spiel, I followed up by emailing the committee's chairperson with links to trade groups, professional societies, and major vendors who would do the development for them. At year's end, I made sure that each group so evangelized received a copy of *America's Strategy for STEM Education,* with my request to circulate it throughout their community.

A year in one of Earth's most iconic cities meant hosting visitors every couple weeks. I lost track of the number of National Mall monument walks; White House tours; Georgetown restaurants; National Cathedral services; Arlington Changing of the Guard Ceremonies; expeditions to The Wharf; Art, History, and Science Museum strolls; and Reagan Airport receptions I'd coordinated for guests. Practically none of it was conducive to meeting the mission, except to help maintain my sanity. Pat's advice rang in my ear—for this not to be remembered as the year Jeff was gone, but as the year of revelry in DC, for friends and family. And did we revel.

The Washington Wizards were a mediocre NBA basketball team playing in the Capital One Arena straight east from me, down F Street, about two and a half miles. Astoundingly talented rock and jazz bands would play the main concourse before games, themselves worth the price of admission. And food options in the arena included world-class Asian chicken, artisanal burgers, and Greek cuisine, to be washed down by any of the twenty-one brands of brew offered at self-serve beer kiosks. Another two and a half miles south of Capital One Arena is the home of an up-and-down major league baseball team, the Nationals. In their down year of 2018, I became a big fan of two supremely athletic human beings on the roster—Bryce Harper, a power-hitting outfielder who was traded away that year to the Phillies, for what was then the richest contract in pro sports history. And ace pitcher Max Scherzer, who—wouldn't you know it—would lead the team to the World Series Championship in 2019, after I'd left.

As with pregame entertainment at Wizards games, my guests might argue that pregame at the Nationals was their highlight. We would ride the DC Metro's Green Line to the game, exit at Navy Yard, and ascend the stairway half a block north of the ballpark, on Half Street, literally. And right there, amid gleaming glass and chrome high-rise condominiums, is a seemingly abandoned parking lot enclosed by stacked cargo shipping containers, with an entryway bearing a marquee reading, *The Bullpen*. Inside, the perimeter would be lined with food trucks and beverage vendors. Big-screen TVs stood against open sky above, and a stage hosting the mid-Atlantic's best live bands took up the north side. We lingered there well into the third and fourth innings, sometimes before guilt over ticket investments would nudge us over to the ballgame. The Bullpen would remain packed.

For my non-sporting visitors, the Kennedy Center was a ten-minute walk down Virginia Avenue. Most afternoons of the week, one could find local live entertainment—concerts, plays, comedy troupes—as well as major Broadway performances like *Hamilton* and *Miss Saigon*. But a most pleasant surprise there was the dining. The KC Cafe and the Roof Terrace Restaurant offered the most surprisingly affordable and upscale surf, turf, and fowl cuisine. The vista while dining on the terrace spanned Alexandria over the Potomac, Georgetown to the west, and Foggy Bottom to the east.

Rooftop bars and restaurants are a thing in DC, and we took in plenty, including the Watergate Hotel's Top of the Gate next door; the Hotel Hive back up the hill, overlooking George Washington University; and the boutique Embassy Row Hotel's rooftop lounge overlooking Dupont Circle.

The cool winds of autumn drove us off the rooftops, and visitor frequency tapered off in the fall, mercifully. As the final push approached, weekdays and weekends blurred while I prepared to run the gantlet of clearances between Halloween and Thanksgiving that would decide my fate.

9

FOURTH-QUARTER CRUNCH

Six hundred nominations poured into the National Science Foundation, from all sectors of the STEM education spectrum across the country. CEOs of major nonprofits. Leaders of some of the nation's most populous school districts. Distinguished academics. Decorated teachers. Business executives. Science center directors. Many nominations had come with support letters from members of Congress.

It had been two years since former President Obama signed the American Innovation and Competitiveness Act, which required that a citizens' panel of STEM experts be established to oversee federal STEM activities. By early spring of 2018, the tetrad of agencies assigned to create the panel—NOAA, ED, NASA, and NSF (lead)—began sifting through the list. I was invited to take part in their weekly meetings as an observer and occasional commenter, and this I can assure any American nominee or selectee: These four agencies created an elaborate and thorough algorithm for consideration that balanced a constellation of factors, including gender, race, ethnicity, leadership in STEM, and cross-sectional representation across the palette of stakeholder groups. The only gap in the array of eventual appointees, numbering eighteen, was community college representation—the skilled technical sector. With no one from that sector, my sales pitch to the group would prove to be less smooth.

Their first assemblage in Washington, DC, was scheduled for September 12, 2018, at the NSF. The panel's first duty was to review and comment on our federal STEM plan, by then nearly fully baked. It was the penultimate hurdle between me and done, followed only by the interagency final sign-off process—called an LRM, for reasons explored shortly.

An icebreaker was held at a restaurant in Alexandria, on Tuesday evening, the 11th, attended by most of the appointees, as well as representatives of the four agencies. Among them was the director of the NSF, who expressed deep gratitude for their willing service. I mingled and met as many as I could, hoping to soften any hidden intentions to stir up trouble the next day. The stakes were so high at that point I was full-on paranoid.

Back at Studio 505 that night, I felt sanguine about the next day.

At 6:30 a.m., Wednesday, Corey and I met at the Farragut West Metro stop for the Blue Line back to NSF. We had the outbound train to ourselves—the flow was inward to DC, light at that time of day. Corey wanted to use the forty-five-minute ride to go over talking points and rehearse the sequence of events that had brought us to this point. I preferred closed-eyes meditation, swaying with the rhythm of the rails. We both did our things.

The meeting began at 8:00 a.m. after a continental breakfast, where I strove to greet the late-arriving panelists who'd missed dinner. The conference room tables were arranged in a long rectangle accommodating fifteen people on the north and south sides and five on both the east and west sides. Someone had laid out cardboard nametags, putting Corey and me at the center of the east end, flanked by FC-STEM members representing NASA and NSF. Opposite us were the co-chairs of the panel who'd been elected via teleconference leading up to the face-to-face meeting. One was an executive at Intel, the other a former NOAA scientist now heading up the National Science Teaching Association.

Seated around the table were panelists from universities, research centers, major corporations, national nonprofits, metropolitan museums, and K–12 schools. We, the four agency reps and I, had spent weeks developing an agenda that essentially sought input on the 2019 STEM plan, section by section. The NSF's Aileen moderated the discussion, inviting me to lead off with an overview of the process and content of the draft strategic plan that they'd been expected to examine before arriving. About a half-hour in, Corey and I found ourselves against the ropes, taking body blows—mostly polite and respectful, yet aggressive—for the remainder of the day.

"Where in this plan do you address America's teacher shortage in high-need areas like math and physics?" scolded a panelist, while leafing through the printed-out draft.

"I'm concerned that this president's budget is weak on science and technology investment, said another. "So what are we to expect in terms of funding for the priorities in this plan?"

"I'm pleased to see that equity is one of three goals of the plan," a panelist said, softly, then leaned forward and boomed, "But that's not enough. This day and age, an overarching commitment to equity and diversity should be the only goal. Everything else is secondary."

"There's plenty of emphasis on workforce readiness and skills development," said a college professor. "But what about the pipeline to scholar and researcher—our MDs and PhDs who discover new knowledge?"

I had miscalculated, thinking the panelists would arrive wide-eyed and demure upon landing such high-altitude seats—that they would listen lots and say little, until maybe their second or third quarterly meeting. I also mistakenly figured they would have fully reviewed the new plan, arriving awestruck by the progress we'd made.

No. They seemed to fully understand the moment in STEM history, and some had marked up, dog-eared, and Post-it-noted their copy of the draft plan with personal pet additions. They came out swinging. Most of their input was constructive and valuable, with a fraction from just a couple of panelists so nitpicky and abrasive that it suggested their politics ran contrary to Corey's, and—they might have presumed—to mine.

Rather than the celebratory rubber-stamping I had hoped for, the panel loaded us down with hundreds of pages of feedback, ranging from wordsmithing to section gutting.

That night, for the third time over the course of that year, I slunk back to Suite 505, fearful of mission failure. This time, my sense of foreboding was even more pronounced than at that shaky first FC-STEM meeting, or the deluged state-federal summit. I did not know what degree of power this panel possessed. Did we need to do everything they wanted? It would require a significant rewrite.

Overwhelmed in the moment, my spirits were buoyed by what had been the closing commentary of an otherwise quiet panelist, a gentleman widely respected across the STEM world: "I think that Jeff and Corey and this team have done a magnificent job."

In the days that followed, Corey provided a valuable presence while we analyzed the mounds of input, deciding what we would change and incorporate, and what we would not. It required the administration's strong arm since the agencies feared complaints getting back to Congress. From hundreds of suggested revisions, he helped us slice and dice the feedback down to a manageable few dozen revisions that STPI and I rewrote over a sleep-deprived week. Placating a main concern of the agency representatives—that panelists might grumble about not being heard—Corey cosigned, alongside NOAA, NASA, ED, and NSF, a letter to each panelist explaining what we changed and did not change, and why. Panelists with whom I've interacted since found that to be respectful and satisfactory.

By golly, I just might make deadline.

"Otto wants a hotwash on Friday morning," Corey told me, a few days after the panel. "And bring STPI."

This would be my second "hotwash" with Otto. He holds one after all significant OSTP events. We'd also had one after the state-federal summit. The first time I heard the term, it sure sounded like an act of hygiene. But I learned that Otto had retained the military lingo from his Navy days. It was a reference to washing down the guns while they're still hot. A debrief.

"I need you guys to map out the next few weeks," Otto said, to lead off his hotwash—not so much cleaning the guns, as planning future battles.

Back in the summer, STPI and I had produced a beautiful Gantt chart, at Otto's request, detailing the processes, checkpoints, and milestones to producing a STEM plan in 2018. But at the time, we'd short-shrifted October through mid-November, simply charted as an arrow densely labeled "Clear FC-STEM, LRM, West Wing, CoSTEM (last)."

Corey and Lydia—whose extraordinary skill in fed-speak writing and editing had, by then, made her part of our inner STEM circle—attended the hotwash, too. Corey stepped to the whiteboard and erased a patch of political graffiti left by the interns—*MAGA, Red Wave, Raised Right*. "OK," he led off, writing, *December...*at the bottom. "Let's pick a debut day, maybe a week before Jeff departs, just in case."

In case what? In case he decides to stick around, after all, or in case a spike jams our gears?

Either way, we all retrieved our calendars and tossed up days in the first week of December. Tuesday the 4th appeared to work, tentatively.

Corey moved his marker up one line. "Good. Now, the final act prior to that will be CoSTEM clearance." Which he scribbled above *December 4th debut*, and added *mid-November*. "And we need to allow for at least a month ahead of that for OMB clearance." Having spent his first decade in DC, at OMB, Corey was handy in navigating that powerful office.

"And we'll need West Wing clearance after that," said Lydia. "Plan for at least a week." She was actively shepherding another strategic plan—*Strategy for American Leadership in Advanced Manufacturing*—through the approval channels just ahead of ours, illuminating our path.

"That puts us at," Corey marked *OMB* and *WW* in parentheses, above the CoSTEM date on the whiteboard, "first or second week of October, we need a final draft, Jeff." That was a couple of weeks away.

"Yikes," I groaned.

I looked over to Liam and Alicia, who, that very week, were deep into wading through input from the citizens' panel. They appeared, as usual, unflapped.

"We still have writing teams redrafting sections, adding citations." I began chronicling our to-do list. "And Lydia and I have only started the executive summary. And—"

"Actually, there's way too heavy a use of citations in the draft as it exists," Lydia said. "It reads like a doctoral dissertation."

That was a cold splash of water. For months, I'd been driving the writing teams hard to present airtight cases for our priorities anchored to irreproachable citations. If only I'd read the other strategic plans that had come out of this administration's OSTP—a cybersecurity R&D strategic plan, a near-Earth object preparedness strategy, and a roadmap for medical imaging research and development. They were scant on citations except for federal references.

"We're making a case for profound shifts in STEM education for the nation," I said. "It needs to be an ironclad, empirically airtight case."

"It is a White House document," Lydia said. "Not some term paper. You are the expert. You've taken the input of countless experts. The White House is not going to judge scholars and their journal articles as citation-worthy or not."

What Lydia was about to advise would shrink the final document to thirty-six pages, thereby fulfilling my forty-page soothsay of nine months earlier. So there was an upside.

"The goals and priorities of this plan need to stand on their own merits. Scrub it of all the non-fed citations."

"And as far as executive summary," Otto said, "I have a guy over at Energy. He's done lots of this kind of thing."

I looked at Lydia, aghast at this notion of farming out a critical piece of the plan. She shrugged and shook her head to say, *Don't worry about it. We have bigger things to focus on.*

"Jeff, I'm going to put him in touch with you," Otto said. "Work with him, please."

I did. And it took multiple drafts reviewed by a dozen sets of eyeballs to get his summary where we wanted it, whereas Lydia and I would have likely spent a weekend knocking it out. It was baffling late-stage meddling by Otto.

By hotwash's end, we compromised on a final draft delivery date of October 10th, when FC-STEM would have its last look. CoSTEM would convene on November 15th to clear it. Then there'd be a release party on December 4th. The thirty-five days in between would have to go flawlessly.

On a crisp and clear October Monday, I bounded out early for a meeting at the Pentagon to be joined there by Corey and the usual cast of characters. With an hour to get to my destination thirty minutes away, I decided to stroll two miles down Constitution Avenue, toward the L'Enfant Metro station across from the Smithsonian Castle, to pick up the Yellow Line across the Potomac. But after just a couple blocks, I entered the crosswalk at the corner of Virginia Avenue, in front of the Organization of American States, when a red Nissan SUV pulled up. A familiar voice rang out from the backseat window.

"Hey, Jeff, want a ride?"

I angled toward the car and made out Corey.

"Well, fancy meeting you here." I peered in to see who was with him.

It was a full Uber, with Lydia and Sam alongside him, and Otto riding shotgun up front. Back in the small third-row seat was Kate, a freshly minted Rice University neuroscience PhD, three weeks into a one-year fellowship at the OSTP. Otto had recently assigned her to our STEM team for backup.

"Got room for me?" I asked Corey.

He pointed me to the far curb and instructed the driver to pull over. He jumped out and tilted his seat up, inviting Kate to take his place after he and I crawled back to the third row.

"We're going to be plenty early." I showed him the time on my phone.

It was 7:05. Our meeting was at 8:00, and traffic was light going out.

"Want to grab breakfast, anyone?"

"Oh, man." Sam cranked his head around. "Have you not been to the Pentagon? Security's intense, and there's always a long line."

Corey nodded. "And if we have a few minutes to wander, artwork lining the halls is as good as any museum." Then his tone shifted from animated to hushed. "And before or after, you've got to see the 9/11 memorial."

With the six of us cruising down I-395, toward Arlington that morning, it was once again reminiscent of a college road trip— spirits were up and chatter light, heading to our first of many LRM— legislative referral memorandum— visits to come. My mind drifted four decades back, to a crowded Chevy Malibu speeding toward Missouri, from our University of Iowa freshman dorm, on a July mission to stock up on fireworks—illegal but highly prized, and permitted right across the southern border. The parallel tickled me—our college mission to the Show-Me State, brimming with expectations of lighting up Independence Day, and our adult junket to the Pentagon, and the agency visits to follow, with expectations to illuminate American education, my own independence of Washington in the balance.

The legislative referral memorandum process comes out of the Office of Management and Budget. Back in September, when our team was projecting a timeline for the completion of the STEM plan, Otto had wondered if we needed to go through LRM.

My ears perked up. "Why? What's LRM?" And most importantly, "How long does it take?"

All eyes turned to Corey—they all deferred to him on this decision, given his OMB heritage.

"Oh, it could range from a couple of weeks to months," he told me.

Reflexively I hated the idea and pooh-poohed it, whatever it was. They ignored me.

"Uhh, umm." Corey wrestled with the necessity for LRM, eyebrows bent in empathy toward me. "Yeah, we really do need to do it. Otherwise, it leaves us vulnerable to somebody in Congress or an agency pulling the plug right up until December fourth, 2018."

Begrudgingly, I accepted the unforeseen hurdle, urging Corey and Otto to get the wheels in motion, whatever that might entail.

The OMB conducts the LRM process for new congressional legislation—or in this case, executive office policy directives—that impact others in the federal government. The STEM plan would be uploaded into the OMB's legislative information system. Then Senate and House leadership, agency directors, and White House policy advisors would get notified to go in and review it for approval. It sounded fraught with risk. Anyone in that array could click a decline button and kill the plan?

Highly unlikely, said Corey. The bigger worry was how long it can take agency heads to circulate the document throughout their dominion before clicking *Approve*.

"Let's just say," Corey said, "they don't share your urgency. And some who we'll need to clear this, don't share this administration's priorities. That'd manifest as stalling."

Since posing the LRM question, Otto had stood at the window, looking down on tourists meandering along Pennsylvania Avenue.

Now, he spun around. "I'll clear this with Leo, but consider a full-court press."

"There you go," Lydia purred.

Only, she must've known what he meant.

For us, the puzzled, he elaborated. "We invite ourselves to all ten CoSTEM agencies for a personal walk-through and verbal commit."

The idea of these supremely busy public servants devoting that kind of time to my niche specialty evoked a brew of mixed emotions—humbled, embarrassed, honored, and proud. Looking back now, they were more about notching a win for the administration than about me. Either way, I'd take it.

―⁂―

Security check at the Pentagon went remarkably smooth—Sam noted the new kiosks lined up for us each to slide in our federal personal identity verification cards for admission. No other agency had progressed to that state of technology yet. Whenever I visited the others, whether NASA, NOAA, ED, EPA, Interior, NSF, or whomever, I joined the line with the tourists for a shoes, belt and bag X-ray and magnetron gate—it mattered not one bit that I had a White House Personnel Identification Verification (PIV) around my neck. I sometimes longed to stay with the tour groups and just browse, exit, then go home.

With twenty minutes to spare, Corey advised we stroll the outer of the five rings of hallways making up the six-million-square-foot structure, and take in the gorgeous military paintings. There were depictions of World War I biplane air battles, heroic images of nurses caring for the injured, Cold War-era missiles poised in silos somewhere in Montana, and President George H. W. Bush pinning a Medal of Honor on a weathered old Marine still able to fit into his Korean War dress blues. We did not have time to check out the 9/11 memorial. Maybe after the LRM visit, Corey said.

By 7:58 a.m., we wound up back at the office of the deputy assistant secretary of the Army, the Defense Department's assigned representative to CoSTEM. I assume she got the assignment because she had expressed or demonstrated a passion for STEM. In our few encounters, she struck me as keenly interested in our work, citing her own kids' tech interests.

The door swung open, and a receptionist greeted us, then led the way to a small boardroom with a wall-sized window, dark green and blast-resistant, overlooking a vast parking lot. Only offices of the outer E ring have windows to the outside world.

Within a couple minutes, the deputy walked in, followed by her representative on the FC-STEM, the Army's research lab director, with whom I had worked closely. We all stood to greet them, Otto particularly swiftly and stiffly. The deputy assistant secretary took the open seat at the head of the table while her lab director and his assistants sat in perimeter chairs. As we'd planned beforehand, Otto opened with the LRM that was underway for clearing the STEM plan—our presence today being an act of support for that process. Corey followed by asserting the administration's strong support for STEM education generally, and this plan specifically. Sam then commented on the favorable reception of Representative Lamar Smith, chairman of the House Science Committee, to our draft plan. Lydia then spoke to the alignment of the STEM plan with her upcoming advanced manufacturing plan, as well as recently released reports on cybersecurity, quantum information science, and near-Earth object preparedness. I followed with an update of what had happened since we'd last convened the CoSTEM in July—incorporation of summit feedback, significant revisions as an outcome of the federal panel of citizens in September, and various content additions and deletions by the writing teams toward refinement. Kate, our new teammate there for backup, listened intently and took copious notes.

"The modern American defense enterprise is deeply and increasingly dependent on STEM-educated soldiers," the deputy responded when she finally had a chance. "And I can't thank Stewart and his team enough," she looked back at the FC-STEM member seated behind her, "for all their work on FC-STEM to get this document to where it is. I think this is a powerful plan that'll shape federal STEM and the practice of STEM education throughout the country for years to come."

Our first LRM is going swimmingly, I indulged in thinking.

Otto asked the deputy assistant secretary if she had any questions.

"Yes, actually." She scanned each of us. "Who can tell me how this plan will change what we do—what Stewart and his team do—to support STEM presently?"

Corey seized the moment. "I think the biggest thing that Defense and other CoSTEM agencies are going to need to attend to," —we were riveted, having not rehearsed for Q&A— "is aligning your STEM spending to new presidential priorities."

I probably would not have dived into the deep end—budget—at this time. Why stir up pushback during LRM? But the budget guy had chosen to ram his point home.

"And if not, you're aware that OMB will catch it in a passback."

A passback, as I had learned months earlier, is OMB rejection of an agency's budget. It's a homework redo—*get your funding right, by the president's goals*. I was over-the-moon happy to learn that OMB would hold agencies accountable for spending in line with our STEM plan. My year in DC would not be wasted on producing merely a dust-collecting federal report.

I would have preferred, however, that reminders about passback be held until we were cleared.

The deputy scowled. "How dramatic a shift does this represent? Stewart, the wonderful work of your team—scholarships, camps, robotics competitions..."

Stewart rose to assure the deputy assistant secretary that their work would change little, though there would need to be greater emphasis on evaluation, especially documenting diverse participants in programs. That's big, yet there's much more to it, I silently channeled through a glare at Stewart. But he'd calmed his boss—priority one, in the moment.

The receptionist poked her head through the cracked doorway to alert the deputy to her 9:00 a.m., just minutes away. We rose and exchanged pleasantries on our way out. Otto waved us all ahead, lingering to ask the Department of Defense's CoSTEM member if we could count on her LRM approval before long.

"You'll have it tomorrow," I heard her say.

So that is how it works. A weight eased off my shoulders.

Corey rushed me in the hallway to apologize for almost mucking it up. He told us he was kicking himself for going all OMB on them, unnecessarily causing concern. It would not happen again, he promised. And by the way, he needed to get back to the Eisenhower Building. So sorry. No time to look at the 9/11 memorial.

I'd never get back to the Pentagon.

Nearly twice a week for the next four, the six of us—or sometimes slight variants of the six, substituting Rick for Sam, or Dylan for Kate—caught an UberXL outside the 17th Street White House gate, bound for CoSTEM members and their STEM teams at the Department of Labor, Education, NASA, Energy, USDA, NIH, and Smithsonian. The only exception was NOAA, whose CoSTEM member met us at the Commerce Department right across 15th Street, from The Ellipse south of the White House. Too bad—I would've enjoyed the long ride with this team to Maryland. The strategy we had enacted at Defense worked well, except no one got into passback.

By the time of the last CoSTEM assembly of my tenure, on November 15th, all but two agencies had approved of the plan through LRM, thanks to our full-court press. To seal the deal, we asked Leo, as co-chair of CoSTEM, to help us out with the stragglers. After the meeting, itself a formality of unanimous public votes of affirmation for the STEM plan, he held up the two delinquent members to ask about the status of their LRM approval, far more important than a verbal affirmation. Both took care of it later that afternoon. We cleared the LRM.

On November 19th, a new committee came into existence: Rick's rollout planning group. Members were a familiar lot—Otto, Corey, Bethany, Sam, Dylan, Kate, and me, chaired by Rick, the OSTP's communications chief. We met twice ahead of Thanksgiving, and every day the last week of November. We drafted press releases, social media posts, and communication chains. I navigated in a state of exhausted satisfaction, a lightheaded euphoria. Only a colossal blunder could botch the mission now. Here came two opportunities.

Rick, working with the White House press office, decided this occasion warranted a media teleconference call. A sneak peek at our shimmering North Star. Invitations were extended to editors and reporters of outlets that typically cover federal science and technology policy—magazines including *Science*, *Nature*, *American Scientist* and *Public Library of Science*; and the journals of professional societies, including the American Physical Society, the American Chemical Society, the Mathematical Association of America, the American Geophysical Union, the National Academies of Sciences, Engineering, and Medicine, the Society of Hispanic Professional Engineers, the Institute of Electrical and Electronics Engineers, and more. Additionally, he invited some from my own list: the National Science Teaching Association, the National Association of Biology Teachers, the Computer Science Teachers Association, the National Council of Teachers of Mathematics, the International Technology and Engineering Education Association, the Afterschool Alliance, the International Society for Technology in Education, and the Association of Science and Technology Centers. I had not seen his full roster of invitees, but heard the number eighty.

"Good morning, and welcome to an exclusive preview of the upcoming release of the president's strategic plan for strengthening STEM education across federal government and throughout the nation," Rick began, following a run of show we'd finalized fifteen minutes earlier.

It was Monday morning, the 3rd of December, exactly twenty-four hours before the document's public debut. Rick introduced himself and acknowledged some of the higher-profile publications represented on the call, then introduced Leo.

"We appreciate everyone's interest in today's topic," Leo said, to launch his opening remarks, which quoted directly from the plan's introduction. "Science, technology, engineering, and mathematics—STEM—have been the foundation for discovery and technological innovation throughout American history. Americans with a strong foundation in STEM have electrified the nation, harnessed the power of the atom, put men on the Moon and rovers on Mars, developed the Internet, designed computers that fit in your pocket, created imaging machines that reveal the inner workings of the body, and decoded the human genome. These stunning achievements have transformed the human experience, inspired generations, and fostered the strong public support for STEM education and research."

That was the first time I had heard our introduction—or any section of the plan, for that matter—read out loud. Although I would not choose Leo for a books-on-tape recording for download—he had a tired, nasal voice—I was pleased with how good our narrative sounded.

A couple years back, a trio of Nashville songwriters had performed their major hits at my university's theater: "Out Last Night," made famous by Kenny Chesney; "Jesus, Take the Wheel," which landed Carrie Underwood a Grammy Award; and more. Between songs, one of them reflected on the out-of-body experience of hearing their song, their personal creation, sung by someone else, broadcast on country radio. Leo reading my work gave me a grain of a notion of their experience.

Leo wrapped up his segment, attempting to convince the journalists of the many great things done by this president to push the frontiers of American science and technology innovation. Then he introduced me to highlight key aspects of the 2019–2023 STEM plan, and to take questions.

"How will the president's fiscal year 2020 budget reflect this commitment to STEM education," said a science journalist from one of the professional societies, zeroing right in, "considering that last year he slashed funding for basic research across agencies, only to have those funds restored by Congress?"

I began to assure the reporters that, of course, the goals and priorities of our STEM plan would enjoy budgetary backing of the administration, before noticing Leo across the table—his eyes bugging out, hand sweeping across his neck in a throat-cutting gesture. I looked over at Rick, who was pointing at Leo.

"Uh, let me hand this back to our director," I said.

Leo challenged the reporter's choice of the word *slash* as an apt description for the president's S&T budget, calling it instead *strategic*, incentivizing agencies to do more of what the nation needs, and less wasting of taxpayer money. He continued elaborating on administration accomplishments, talking points that Rick was mouthing along with. He ended with one more invitation for questions, emphasizing that they should be specific to *America's Strategy for STEM Education*. Surprisingly—sadly, to me—there were no more questions. Rick thanked everyone and hung up.

Two hours later, we held a similar conference call, this time with governors' offices. Instead of Rick's arranging and leading the call, staff came upstairs from the Office of Intergovernmental Affairs. They were in daily touch with states, and had invited education policy advisors and state superintendents of education to the briefing. About a dozen states dialed in. The run of show was similar in all but one way—after my highlights on key aspects of the STEM plan, Corey was to handle the Q&A. I'd been demoted.

"Noting a number of changes in direction in what was to be an update to the 2013 federal STEM plan," said a well-informed New England governor's education policy advisor, "I don't see a priority for more STEM teachers included anymore. Has the need gone away, or diminished in importance?"

"You can be assured that we recognize the importance of a skilled and passionate teacher for every STEM learner in the nation," replied Corey. "And this administration supports a variety of solutions to America's teacher shortage in high-demand subjects such as computing and industrial technology." He did not name specific solutions.

Corey and I had fielded this type of question hundreds of times, so I had a pretty good idea what was coming next—a patent quip he had picked up. And I vividly recall where he got it. On our way back to the Eisenhower from the first LRM visit to the Defense Department in October, I had commented to the team that Stewart, the deputy assistant secretary's FC-STEM member, had undersold the degree of changes being called for in the new STEM plan, telling his boss that their work would change little.

"Short-term," I said, "that's fine." It got us the approval. "What if," I asked the bobbing heads while we bounced across the 14th Street bridge into DC, "they plan for simply business as usual?"

"They committed to lots of the priorities in the dot chart," Lydia said.

"Stewart and others helped a ton with narrative around the new priorities," said Otto. "I don't think you have to worry about buy-in."

"Well, maybe they'll just add your priorities to their current portfolio—no harm, no foul," Sam said.

And then Kate, who'd been upgraded to the front seat next to the Uber driver, turned. I was surprised she could hear the conversation, and was curious what the demure and impeccably mannered new teammate might offer up. She scooched counterclockwise on the bench seat to face us more squarely.

"If everything becomes a priority," she said, softly, "then nothing really is."

Corey had been glum since complicating the Defense LRM meeting, but here he livened up. He loved the pithy aphorism, and instantly adopted it. To the state policy advisor's question on the December 3rd teleconference, he capped his response with, "Yet if we make everything that is important to America's STEM community a priority in this plan, then nothing's a priority. These are the areas that the community believes we need to double down on at this time in history."

Rick launched a social media storm on the morning of December 4th, starting with a press release that I thought to be bombastically titled "America Will Win the Global Competition for STEM Talent." My opinion was not sought. It was posted to the White House Facebook page, as well as the OSTP's Twitter feed, and distributed through news and S&T organizations. My phones—both the White-House-issued iPhone and my personal android—began pinging over breakfast and did not let up. Texts, voicemails, and emails poured in from friends, colleagues, associates, and allies from across the nation—some cheery, others lofty, and still others downright tear-jerking. For example:

> I have never experienced a project of
> the magnitude and importance to be
> conducted in such an open, transparent,
> and inclusive manner. Bringing together so
> many stakeholders from all avenues of STEM
> education not only strengthened the design
> of the report, but also created ownership
> which will only reap benefits as the
> report is released and disseminated.
>
> —A former federal agency contributor,
>   now an education think-tank director

This is a wonderful document that will guide actions and make an impact for a long time to come.

> —An industry executive who'd offered input on the technology sections

---

All Americans have a stake in the success of this initiative.

> —A university president

...what a wonderful piece of work.... I personally love the chart on Page vii.

> —A regional STEM organization CEO

My team and I...have reviewed the report—very glad to see the commitment to diversity and inclusion, as well as to strategic partnerships.

> — A philanthropic foundation manager of STEM portfolio

...the strategy report is very exciting. I'm pleased to see a comprehensive focus on innovation skills, lifelong learning, and the breadth of learning environments and experiences that comprise a person's education over the years.

    —Director of a metropolitan science center

Your team has earned applause and recognition. My gratitude for guiding this important work to what really is more of a starting gate than the finish line.

    —Outreach coordinator for a major technology company

Regardless of what's between the covers of the Plan, which I'm sure will serve the field and the government well in the years to come, this task was Herculean and you handled it with grace and wisdom. The number of cats you had to herd were beyond counting, and here we all are—with a document that will give our STEM education community our North Star. Congratulations again. I know you'll return home feeling exhausted, but I hope there will be some pride and exhilaration mixed in, too. You have accomplished something truly big!

    —Education consultant at a global nonprofit

Just wanted to take a minute and say, "Well-done." I imagine you put roughly one hour per word into this over the past year, and it really shows. Exactly what I was hoping for, and exactly what I think the country needs.

— President of a national STEM education professional society

Printed copies of the only press run of America's Strategy for STEM Education await attendees to the public debut on Tuesday morning, December 4, 2018, in Room 350 of the Eisenhower Executive Office Building.

By 10:00 a.m., guests began arriving at Room 350, for the celebratory debut. Of the 120 seats, I was permitted to fill fifteen of them. Most were the heads of DC-based professional societies and organizations, including the Association of Public and Land-grant Universities, the American Association for the Advancement of Science, the Mathematical Association of America, the National

Association of Manufacturers, the US Chamber of Commerce, the STEM Education Coalition, the National Academies of Sciences, Engineering and Medicine, and STEMconnector®. Each had offered valuable input to the plan. I cherished this chance to repay them.

The others were filled by federal officials across the agencies, including members of CoSTEM and FC-STEM, STPI, contributing writers, citizens advisory panelists, executive office colleagues at the OSTP, representatives from OMB, Domestic Policy Council Intergovernmental Affairs, as well as congressional staff, West Wing representatives, and a few reporters.

I welcomed the assemblage and moderated a trio of speakers to the lectern—first, Leo of the OSTP, then the administrator of NASA, followed by the director of the NSF, each of whom sang praise for the new plan. Two panels of commentators followed—one a group of outsiders, and the other insiders—members of CoSTEM. The outsiders bolstered the North Star function of the plan by telling us all how it would shape programs and philanthropy at a major technology company, at an organization of state directors of education departments, and at a professional society of science teachers. The CoSTEM panelists regaled the plan for setting a clear and ambitious course for their own STEM endeavors. Then *poof*, it was all over.

When the last of the lingerers high-fived me and left around noon, I gave in to gravity, letting my cheeks sag, belly bulge, and shoulders slouch. I trudged to a safe haven—the Executive Office of the President Library, on the fourth floor. After grabbing the *USA Today* off a rack, with no intention of reading it, I snuck up to the balcony level, pulled a chair to the window overlooking The Ellipse below and Washington Monument in the distance. For the fourth time in my life—the first being my wedding day; the second, the birth of my son; and the third, my doctoral hooding—time stopped.

Mercifully, the president shut down government the next day, enabling me to sleep in. The occasion was the celebration of the life of 41st president, George H. W. Bush, at the National Cathedral that morning, his having passed away the previous Friday. The former president had lain in state at the Capitol since the prior evening, and I could hear from my fifth-floor window at 2020 F Street NW, the sounds surrounding his motorcade as it paraded up Pennsylvania Avenue to 22nd Street NW, for the right turn toward the cathedral. Helicopters, cheering throngs, sirens, horns. The president's executive order closed federal offices and excused all federal employees, except those essential to security or defense, from duty for the day.

With immense respect to Number 41, I behaved as if essential. Coffee with the chief development officer of STEMconnector® at 10:00 a.m.; brunch with the fellows who operate a program called Real World Design Challenge; finishing touches to (what I thought would be) my last quarterly progress report to the GAO; midafternoon tea with Louisianans sharing their Cyber Innovation Center; a reception meet-and-greet at the American Mathematical Society over at the Kimpton Hotel, east of the White House; and late-evening preparation for the next day's hotwash on the debut event, while apprising all known STEM stakeholders and individuals across the country, of *America's Strategy for STEM Education,* posted to the White House website. Those final days were unusual in their usual-ness.

A mandatory annual training session was scheduled for the afternoon of my 364th and final day on the premises, Monday, December 10, 2018. I tried to squirm out, but Otto would not hear it—all feds, especially political appointees, must absolutely take this annual briefing. No exceptions. The topic was the Hatch Act.

"The main provision of the Hatch Act of 1939, amended in 2012," lectured the very pregnant attorney from the Office of Special Counsel over on M Street NW, "prohibits employees in the executive branch of the federal government from engaging in political activity while on duty." She paused for a deep inhale, head and shoulders exaggeratedly arched backward in counterbalance to what must have been a nearly due baby. "It's simple, basically," she said to the dozen of us around the table, some doodling, others seemingly meditating, and I all in the moment as this precious era wound down. "Your chair, your computer, your desk, your pen, your time here is owned by the American people. *All* of them." Her voice tinged with the irritation of one who has had to crack down on more than a few knuckleheads who branded their offices with campaign stickers, or used their government computer for campaign fundraising.

In the weeks preceding that briefing, she might've been the very OSC enforcer who cited six White House officials—the president's deputy press secretary, deputy director of communications, executive assistant to the president, former director of media affairs, press secretary for the vice president, and deputy communications director of the Office of Management and Budget—for violating the Hatch Act by posting partisan pronouncements from government Twitter accounts. And maybe she had dealt with the first lady's press secretary for tweeting the president's campaign slogan from her government Twitter account. Was she the one at OSC who had had to crack down on White House counselor Kellyanne Conway for appearing on *Fox & Friends* to pitch a winner in the Roy Moore vs. Doug Jones US Senate race earlier that year? And perhaps she'd prosecuted the 2017 Hatch Act violations by the White House deputy chief of staff for communications, and the United States ambassador to the United Nations for their tweets campaigning for congressional candidates. A little irritation in the voice of the OSC lawyer was painfully understandable.

The Hatch Act briefing was the perfect send-off gift—exiting the building a couple hours later was much easier after having my sentiments dulled.

Twenty-four hours later, I was on a Cozumel beach, kidnapped by Mary.

On December 10, at 4:40 p.m., I clanged closed the gate of the 17th Street NW entrance to the Eisenhower Executive Office Building for the last time as senior policy advisor for STEM education, Office of Science and Technology Policy, Executive Office of the President.

10

UNPLANNED ENCORE

"Man, what was it like?" said a friend, who hosted a celebratory house party upon my return to Iowa. The gentlemen had assembled in the den with cocktails. Some lit cigars. Our ladies gathered in the dining room across the other side of the kitchen. Mary and I hated the segregation typical at these parties, and often bucked it—she'd crash the boy's club, and I'd mingle with the ladies. But I was trapped on an ottoman, surrounded, beholden.

"It was, uh, intense. I mean, sheesh, umm," I spluttered, regretful not to have formulated a few talking points for this inevitable conversation. It would happen many times over.

"Did you meet the Big Guy?" The hopeful questioner was a retail store manager and fan of the president. They all were—a manufacturing engineer, a computer consultant, a chief finance officer for a real estate company. Each would be very comfortable in a MAGA hat. I wished I could wow them.

"Never got to meet the president," I lamented.

The guys swigged their drinks and puffed their stogies, interest slightly diminished.

"But Ivanka came around sometimes," I offered as consolation, perking them up.

"Oh, yeah? What was she like?" said the engineer.

"Tall." I laughed, unsure whether to furnish my impression of her personality, intellect, or appearance. Instead, I provided a context for our meetings. "She became the de facto West Wing advocate for STEM. She was keen on promoting computing to girls."

The engineer eased back into the overstuffed cushion of the couch and pondered the muted college basketball game on the TV above the fireplace mantel over my head. This wasn't the answer he was looking for.

"So what'd you do there, anyway?" our host said, rephrasing his opening question.

But their wives had been in close contact with mine all year, so this question also confused me. We'd all spent lots of time together before I'd left in the fall of '17. One couple had visited me in DC. Surely, I decided, a literal answer would not be the right answer here. Yet a more figurative accounting of what I did all year was more than I could muster at a lighthearted party.

I used to puzzle at the legendary reticence of military veterans to share tales. My own brother had returned from a tour of duty with the Marine Corps while I was in high school, and my pals and I would hound him for stories, to no avail. He was a steel vault of locked memories. My brief national service pales in comparison with the risky multiyear commitment of soldiers, but I now had an inkling of their tight-lipped-ness. Where to begin? Which parts would be interesting to them? How to compress an episode to something arrestive?

"The, uh, the national STEM plan." I pulled up an image of the cover on my phone and shone it at them one by one, watching faces for signs of recognition.

Several said, "Hmh," as if I were showing an ear of corn partly husked, revealing kernels colorful as M&Ms. Interesting, if you're into that sort of thing.

"Now that you've been on the inside," the CFO looked around the semicircle of guys more than at me, "are things as bad as the media makes out?"

The others chuckled, then quieted. As I was the token academic at these gatherings, my political leanings had long been assumed left of center, yet mysterious to them, carefully guarded by me. Once in a while, someone would dangle bait: "Hey, Jeff, what do the liberal elites think of X?" To which I'd laugh and feign ignorance. We had bonded years ago when I coached our sons' baseball teams. Back when politics was not so polarized nor so central to one's identity. But here was a test of my political allegiance—perhaps a redder conservative now for the experience? This litmus paper of a question would reveal my political leanings, finally.

"I can say this much for sure." I sat up straight on the footstool. Now we'd landed on something I had thought lots about, having been both consumer and subject of the political media lately. I leveraged what the CFO honored as my insider advantage to push the fellows a bit.

"I left the White House grounds on December 10th, two days after the president fired Chief of Staff General Kelly. Attorney General Jeff Sessions was fired a month ahead of Kelly. National security advisor General McMasters resigned in March, and General Mattis quit ten days after I departed. That's five fewer adults in the room. And gents, trust me, the media is holding back on how bad it really is."

My friends rose and stretched, ambled to the kitchen to freshen their drinks, and changed the subject. We've not been invited back.

"Please indulge this request to begin planning for succession," began my email to Leo, copying Otto and the rest of the OSTP leadership team, in October of 2018, "given that approximately sixty days remain of my one-year agreement."

A week later—an eon in STEM time—Leo replied curtly, inviting me to provide a list of successor candidates. I generated a roster of a dozen capable nominees without contacting them for permission.

"Leo," I wrote back, "here are twelve people who would do a magnificent job for you—a couple of rock-star state STEM leaders of similar heritage as myself; six nonprofit executives well-versed in STEM; two commercial vendors widely respected in STEM circles; a business executive passionate about STEM; and a writer/social media influencer with an extensive STEM fan base. Let me know if you'd like to be introduced. None has been informed of my mentioning them to you."

Halloween came with no word from Leo. At a 2:00 p.m. sync-up meeting with Corey, I recounted the exchanges on succession, worried for the OSTP as the clock wound down. Come December and beyond, someone would need to convene FC-STEM monthly, coordinate the interagency working groups, deliver progress reports to GAO and Congress, draw up an implementation plan, review STEM legislation for the executive branch, assist other OSTP teams with the integration of STEM in their reports and strategies, prepare Leo and others for meetings where STEM came up, and who knows, maybe even run a White House STEM festival.

"I checked with Leo," Corey told me, the next day, "and they want some new names." What they'd done to determine the unfitness of the twelve people I'd proposed wasn't a courtesy extended to me. In digging deeper into my network of contacts, I took a stab at heightening the odds of success by leaning into corporate types and red-state STEM leaders exclusively. By November, it was becoming obvious my successor would not be in place by departure day. The OSTP under this administration was prone to reverting to a stalled state vulnerable to audit and noncompliance.

"Let's school up Kate," Cory said to me, after a rollout meeting on November 20th. "She's sharp and really into STEM. And frankly, she's bored."

"Corey, the agencies, not to mention Congress, may likely feel disrespected by a White House that sends up a temporary staffer on fellowship, with no relevant experience to lead the nation's STEM portfolio."

"OK, then, I have a proposal." A wry smile creased his cheeks. He knew I couldn't stay on, but was he about to dash my dwindling hopes for a clean break? "I'll stick very close on the STEM portfolio alongside her if you'd consider giving us just part-time to keep up co-chairing FC-STEM, steering the IWGs, and coaching Kate on reports—she's an excellent writer. The three of us tag-teaming can pull this off until your replacement is found."

"Aw, shoot, Corey," I groaned. "My Iowa team, the governor, I need to—"

"Jeff." He grabbed my forearm. "For your country, I'll fast-track the clearance of your successor. We'll ask Leo, or maybe Ivanka, to phone your governor to keep you on."

All parties eventually agreed to ten hours per week, plus two days back in DC each month, until I was replaced.

That took nine more months.

The longest government shutdown in US history followed me out the door in late 2018. Colleagues within the OSTP and the agencies were among the eight hundred thousand federal workers sent home on December 22nd, awaiting resolution of the funding impasse over the president's Mexico border wall. Five weeks later, on January 25th, all went back to work on a three-week agreement between Congress and the president to strike a compromise, with the president threatening to declare a national emergency to get the money—which he did on February 15th.

Awful as the shutdown was, the dead period gave me time to reestablish my state director post before commencing the OSTP consulting agreement. Although our work may not have qualified as *essential* by shutdown exemption standards, my FC-STEM co-chairs requested that we phone in weekly, anyway, to keep the embers glowing. Corey and Kate asked for a similar arrangement so that, upon the government's reopening, we'd all hit the ground running.

On January 25th, we jump-started the federal STEM engine. Kate revealed an excellent writing aptitude and ready grasp of the swirling forces at work—federally, at least—on STEM education funding and programming. She took the lead on drafting two key documents: a federal implementation plan we'd called for in *America's Strategy for STEM Education* to ensure the wheels kicked into motion across agencies on the goals of our new plan. And a progress report required by Congress midyear. We exchanged iterations every couple evenings for seven weeks until my return to DC, on February 26th, for my first FC-STEM meeting as remote co-chair.

Two outcomes of that meeting profoundly, and favorably, shaped the future of STEM. First, FC-STEM voted unanimously on our recommendation to blend the two projects—implementation plan and progress report—into a streamlined and consolidated, though naggingly drawn-out, product: Progress Report on the Federal Implementation of the STEM Education Strategic Plan, to be released the following fall. Second, and more importantly, the committee launched new interagency working groups to succeed the five we had phased out in December. Almost everyone enthusiastically jumped on one of the IWGs covering the five pathways of our new plan—Strategic Partnerships, Convergence, Computational Literacy, Transparency & Accountability, and Inclusion in STEM. What they would come up with as strategies were swift and resolute—committing their agencies to new dots on the all-important chart appearing as Appendix 1 in the progress report. And they linked their agency STEM programs to our new goals and priorities in a list as Appendix 2 that would from here forward hold everyone accountable to the 2019–2023 STEM plan. Our imprint would stick. The hard work and sacrifice on the part of so many would leave a legacy.

Weekly teleconferences and monthly FC-STEM meetings through spring and summer of 2019 focused on *how* and *when*, no longer *if*. At long last, during our August meeting, I was able to introduce the new senior policy advisor and assistant director for STEM education at the Office of Science and Technology policy. We had a month of onboarding sessions until my final official trip back on September 23rd—briefing FC-STEM on the states, nonprofits, and businesses across the country adopting and aligning their work to our North Star. Kate and I both took our final bow that day.

On the one-year anniversary of the release of our STEM plan, December 4, 2019, the OSTP conducted another STEM summit—this time, just for feds. About a hundred attendees from eighteen agencies came together, intent on supporting the recommendations coming out of the IWGs. By 2020, hundreds of millions of dollars in grant opportunities at the National Science Foundation, the Departments of Education, Defense, Labor, and others were now prominently aligned to goals and priorities of the 2019–2023 plan, fundamentally shaping how colleges, schools, state agencies, and their partners across the nation go about their business.

And finally, in the fall of 2020, the OSTP released through the Federal Register a request for information, a common tool for fact-finding on impressions and impacts of proposed or enacted federal policies. They were, no doubt, curious to learn about the STEM plan's utility among practitioners nationwide to gauge activities and inform an eventual 2024 update.

The most novel and controversial part of *America's Strategy for STEM Education* was its nationwide rallying call. The idea fragmented the feds: Some grasped the potency of our product to synchronize the oars of all the STEM boats rowing across America. Others thought it to be a distracting sideshow. A few opined that we'd taken liberties beyond the congressional intent of the COMPETES Act. And as always, a couple folks were downright vituperative, which I learned, eventually, to dismiss as misdirected political reflex. Had Corey and my OSTP posse disliked it, I would have abandoned ship. But they were starry-eyed about the North Star.

The only metric I had to go by as far as the new plan's value out there was usage. All the battle scars would be worthwhile if the document were to cast ripples across STEM pools of America. But with no budget for dissemination, or for gathering feedback (until the 2020 request for information), I became both town crier and census taker. At least, initially. Through late 2019 and early 2020, my habit of leisurely browsing the agendas of STEM-related conferences and summits across the country would occasionally, when I'd spot a presentation or a keynote on our strategic plan, send a 100-volt jolt through my body. An FC-STEM member, or a citizens' advisory panelist, or one of our contributors would get it onto the program somewhere. I'd nearly swallow my uvula.

One day, back at my home office in Iowa, a flyer arrived in the mail from a scientific supply company—the sort of bulk mailing we in science get all the time. This one summarized our five-year STEM plan for customers. I would have hugged the salesperson from Pitsco had she shown up in my hall. Gloriously, it was the first of many.

A summary of
Charting a Course for STEM Success:
America's Strategy for STEM Education

Commercial vendors gave our STEM plan a lift by promoting it to customers and generating supportive manuals, kits and curricula aligned to it.

"Please let me know the level of awareness of—maybe even alignment to, or adoption of—the goals and priorities of *America's Strategy for STEM Education* at your [local/regional/state/national] organization," I emailed to every imaginable STEM executive I could think of across the USA, in early 2019. Basically, my own personal RFI.

Over the following months, scores of inspiring testimonials rolled in. A number of organizations such as STEMx, the Teaching Institute for Excellence in STEM, the Council of State Science Supervisors, the National Council of Teachers of Mathematics, and others wrote back that they were holding webinars, posting in newsletters, and featuring at their conferences word of the plan for their members. Numerous state STEM leaders from Michigan, Arkansas, Wisconsin, South Carolina, Kansas, and more were drafting or amending state strategic plans aligned to our North Star. Businesses and foundations, like Texas Instruments and the Tiger Woods Foundation, were tying their investments to programs supporting the plan. My monthly returns to Washington for FC-STEM meetings regularly included on the agenda updates from beyond the Beltway. My federal colleagues appeared equally jazzed about the nationwide buzz, even those who had been harsh critics.

Invitations for me to come share the story of our STEM plan began to accumulate in the waning days of 2018, dramatically picking up through 2019 into 2020. A dozen state STEM summits from Missouri to Virginia asked my full dose of our North Star. STEM advocacy conferences focused on equity and workforce, and regional networks invited me on stage for briefings on *America's Strategy for STEM Education*. Professional education societies with concentrations as varied as agriculture, cybersecurity, and ecology were eager to hear my advice about how they could plug into and benefit from our plan.

Then on March 12, 2020, I was in Baltimore to present the keynote address to the International Technology and Engineering Educators Association, when the conference was shut down after breakfast. We were all sent home on account of a novel virus spreading across the continent. The next day I was to fly to North Dakota's STEM summit which got canceled as well. All went quiet.

Today, an Internet search of *Charting a Course for Success: America's Strategy for STEM Education* nets tens of millions of results. Although most of the links now aim at the expired OSTP website of the 45th administration, it remains available on Eric.ed.gov and Amazon.com, as well as the documents archive of the 45th administration Office of Science and Technology Policy. My new pet peeve is the rare communication with a distinguished STEM scholar, administrator, or policymaker unaware of, or maybe ignoring, our seminal document. Ah, to have so little to worry about.

By no later than the fall of 2023, either congress will have rewritten the COMPETES Act, deleting STEM, or a presidential administration will have found an OSTP senior policy advisor for STEM education to update our strategic plan. Did the bar we set fulfill its potential as a model, as the OSTP director predicted to me, below, in 2019?

> The STEM plans are the best this Nation has ever seen, and great progress already is being made owing to your vision and tenacity. The STEM effort set a high bar for engaging the broad community, and is now a role model...

The new administration elected in 2020 needed their own leading thinker in STEM to take up the task of renewal. An update to our STEM plan hopefully finds it a dependable compass upon which everyone can rely as a nonpartisan, pragmatic guide to policy and practice. The nation must beware, though, a pedigreed insider assigned to the STEM portfolio, brilliant no doubt, but bereft of the street cred born of authentic experience in STEM. That is a recipe for irrelevance. A mere exercise.

And if my successor's successor casts the broadest net to solicit the input of the widest possible cross-section of stakeholders, the updated goals and priorities are likely to be custom fitted to the ever-evolving needs of learners, workplaces, and communities. But beware again, a product hatched from inside Washington—a surprise holiday gift sprung upon the STEM community—will be as stale as Grandma's holiday fruitcake upon arrival.

American STEM education is rapidly evolving beyond the basic intent of the COMPETES Act—to make more engineers, scientists, data analysts, and computer programmers. Having begun as a workforce initiative, STEM has surprised no one more than its agents on the ground who, like young wizards of Hogwarts, discover by accident, through practice the power they possess.

STEM education necessarily transcends the disciplines. It's become a vehicle by which schools reconnect to communities. It's forced educators to rethink what and how they teach, abandoning lectures and lock-step curriculum in favor of finding and solving problems. Future updates of *America's Strategy for STEM Education* may well not focus on STEM, but on skills of a successful employee and citizen—critical thinker, data analyzer, predictor, collaborator, innovator. A future reauthorization of COMPETES might, appropriately, switch out every mention of *STEM* for *innovation*, and thereby keep right up with the times.

The occupant of my OSTP chair will have a golden opportunity to usher in the next evolution with an update, *America's Strategy for Innovation Education*. May this book provide them with aid and insight into getting there. May it stand as a shining instance of nonpartisan collective impact against the backdrop of roiling seas of political discord. May the politicians take a lesson—turn it over to the experts and get out of the way.

EPILOGUE

All of the 2016-2020 political appointees to the OSTP have my sympathy. Most of them were younger than I. That goes for all of the Obama-era OSTP staffers I'd met over coffee in 2018, too. Where do you go after the White House? How do you follow that act? It's all downhill from there.

Many of them landed decent jobs at think tanks and institutes in DC. When you exit the White House gates, lots of job offers come forth. But it wasn't hard to slink back to the corn rows of Iowa after a stint in the limelight, when it was merely the cherry atop a well-defined career. Most of these folks had gotten the cherry without earning a sundae upon which to perch it. A forlornness colored the demeanor of former staffers, which I knew would be in store for Bethany and Dylan, Rick, Corey, Leo, and other appointees before too long.

I hardly came through it untouched, though.

As much as I left a mark on American STEM education, the job left an indelible mark on me, too. Lots of marks, actually—both good and bad. For example, once you've surfed the crest, self-doubt is extinguished. There's no longer any challenge or problem intimidating enough to chase you off the wave. The opposite—after the incessant pressure of riding the crest, it's easy to get bored. My favorite part of work these days comes when a crisis arises, inducing that familiar adrenaline rush perfusing my veins to heighten the senses and quicken the pulse. Alongside that confidence, or maybe fueling it, is the indubitable validation of one's thinking. My ideas about STEM education were tried in the highest court and held to be valid. So I've got that going for me, which is nice, to borrow a line from Carl the groundskeeper in the movie *Caddyshack,* after caddying for the Dalai Lama.

On the downside, I came out of there aged. Internet memes of Obama, Bush, Clinton, and Reagan before and after they served document the well-known phenomenon. After less than two years inside, I advanced more than five years physically, though friends and family kindly euphemize the morph as appearing "wiser." An easy trade.

Not so easy, nor so measurable a trade-off, is the academic ding I may have incurred. Before accepting the OSTP appointment, I had read about the damaged reputations and impugned character of academics who had signed on with the 2016–2020 presidential administration, widely recognized as anti-science. I had openly worried to my friend Jerry, at the Iowa-versus-Illinois football game back in October of 2017, about that sort of fallout. Acknowledging the risk, he rightly advised taking it anyway. To not engage would leave God-knows-who in charge of STEM. By this dimension, I took one for the team, despite struggling more lately, it seems, to land peer-reviewed grants and publish peer-reviewed work. It could be, of course, that my work is subpar and that I am blinded by that new confidence of having ridden the crest.

Still, my professional network is exponentially greater. I'm more humble after almost infantile dependency on countless experts teaching me to crawl at the OSTP, then walk, then run across the finish line. But that all left me tired, and I'm still waiting to get back to pre-OSTP vigor. And despite the ugliness that colors politics today, I'm more optimistic about Washington's capacity to lead us, only because of those national treasures—career employees—working hard within the agencies.

"How in heaven's name did you get anything done in that dysfunctional administration?" said my New Deal Democratic mother, recently.

"Because, Mom," I replied, "two layers down from that Oval Office drama are brilliant, selfless, mostly nonpartisan civil servants (as she was) keeping the wheels of government turning, despite wacky elections."

Above all that, though, towering over all the marks left on me, is a new appreciation for home. I'd taken for granted the bucolic Grant Wood-ness of Iowa's landscape, the unpretentious openness of its people, and the quiet calm of its mornings and nights. No longer.

Summing it all up, I took the excellent advice of the rapper Eminem and recommend that anyone with a passion fueled by preparation do the same if, and when, a big door opens. Paraphrasing from "Lose Yourself:"

> *This opportunity comes once in a lifetime.*
>
> *You only get one shot.*
>
> *You better lose yourself in the moment.*
>
> *You better never let it go, yo.*

ABOUT THE AUTHOR

Jeff Weld directs Iowa's widely acclaimed statewide STEM education program on behalf of the governor. A decorated college professor, scholar, and former high school teacher, Jeff frequently writes for, speaks to, and strategizes with groups aspiring to unleash the transformative power of STEM education at the national, state, and local levels. In late 2017, he accepted a White House invitation to join the Executive Office of the President as senior policy advisor for STEM education in the Office of Science and Technology Policy. In defiance of the natural order of federal policymaking, it took him just twelve months to fulfill a promise to lead the production of *America's Strategy for STEM Education*, a nonpartisan five-year plan to guide federal agencies and to rally the nation around STEM education.

Returning to the helm at Iowa's STEM program in 2019, Jeff continued to serve the Office of Science and Technology Policy part-time for nine more months, helping to develop federal strategies that translate lofty STEM policies into practical, measurable and impactful federal agency programs. He takes the reader along behind the scenes and between the lines on a twenty-one-month adventure imbued with personal and policy intrigue, illuminating the shadows of American education policy-setting.

Connect with Jeff at:

facebook.com/jeff.weld.1
instagram.com/jeffweld
Twitter: @JdWeld
Linkedin: jeffrey-weld-b868345
weldwrites.com

www.ingramcontent.com/pod-product-compliance
Lightning Source LLC
Chambersburg PA
CBHW031259110426
42743CB00041B/740